1,2,3,5,6

teaching
second edition

from the outside in

Larry Beauchamp
Gerald McConaghy
Jim Parsons
Kathy Sanford
Dawn Ford

Second Edition 5 4 3 2

copyright © 2000 Les Éditions Duval, Inc.

Duval House Publishing/Les Éditions Duval, Inc.

Head Office:
18228 - 102 Avenue
Edmonton, Alberta
CANADA T5S 1S7
Telephone: (780) 488-1390
Fax: (780) 482-7213
Toll-free: 1-800-267-6187
E-mail: pdr@compusmart.ab.ca
Website: www.duvalhouse.com

Typeset by Pièce de Résistance Ltée.
Printed and bound in Canada by Quality Color Press

 We acknowledge the financial support of the Government of Canada through the Book Publishing Industry Development Program (BPIDP) for our publishing activities.

Canadian Cataloguing in Publication Data

Main entry under title:

Teaching from the outside in

ISBN 1-55220-200-3

1. Teaching. I. Beauchamp, Larry, 1943-
LB1025.3.T42 2000   371.102   C00-911533-1

CONTENTS

PREFACE

So you're going to be a teacher. And, at least to this point, no one has been able to talk you out of it with stories of complex children, difficult parents, poor salaries, endless planning, hours of grading and lack of respect. Good. You are the kind of people for whom we are looking. You have already made a crucial first decision about being a good teacher — you haven't given up.

The fact that no one has talked you out of teaching puts all of us in the same boat. We, too, are long-time teachers. We've taught collectively for over 100 years. The point is that somehow we have at least developed a way to survive the institution, the culture, and the people of schools. You may be surprised, but there are many people similar to us — people who love teaching. No, not every day is a great day, but we hang in there. And we usually have a good time.

What will you find in this book? We will give you much advice. So, here's our first bit. If you are going to be a teacher, you have to figure out a way to have a good time. It's simple: if you can't have a good time, you can't survive. Not in the long term, anyway. We believe that, similar to any job, the primary way to have a good time in teaching is to become very good at what you do. We want to help you become good at being a teacher. Your task, now that you have made the decision to be a teacher and you aren't going to back down, is to be as good a teacher as you can learn to be.

Did somebody make you buy this book; or did you pick it up on your own because it looked helpful or interesting? It doesn't really matter that much. Either way, we think that this book can help you reach your quest. We began working on this book because we decided, after listening to our students talk about the books they were reading, to put together a book filled with practical ideas and straight talk about teaching. Our students told us that the books they were reading were too "thick," both in terms of pages and in terms of theory. They were sure that the "books would help them later," but they "needed to survive" in the classroom first. The books they were reading might be good, but they weren't helping them "now." We hope to help people now.

So that's where we are coming from. We have tried to write a book that will help aspiring and inexperienced teachers survive in the classroom now. We haven't ignored theoretical aspects of teaching or curriculum, but we have focused on "right now."

In writing this book, we started with the most fundamental activities of teaching — things such as planning, discipline, evaluation, and how students learn — and we tried to discuss each in clear, understandable ways. Then we tried to ask and answer questions that had plagued us when we were young teachers. We included common situations that we had faced in teaching. We talked to our teacher friends and got their ideas about what should be included in a practical, helpful book. And we listened to their experiences.

We hope that including lessons learned from our and others' teaching experiences can help you think about what you will "face" as you teach. We have tried to listen carefully to the needs of our students and to offer responsive ideas that are practical, ready to use, workable and helpful for young teachers.

What you have in this book is experience — not a third-person collected experience from library shelves, but our own experience. We have only written about things that we know or have learned from working with young people in classrooms. This is a book of "how to" activities and concrete down-to-earth hints, methods, and useful ideas sometimes inspired from our mistakes. You will find some theory and hopefully much inspiration.

We have titled this book *Teaching from the Outside In* for several reasons. First, we believe that one way to learn is to work through material and ideas while thinking about what happens. We know that you can't always think about everything before it happens — a sort of "from the inside out" way. Sometimes you just watch things happen — the outside — and try to figure out why they work. Sometimes, without even thinking about it, things just make sense. Educational researchers call this unconscious way of learning "situated cognition." Sometimes things happening on the outside become your inspiration for new teaching ideas. A moment in the school hallway watching the energized exchanges between students, a glance or smile in the cafeteria from one of your ESL students, or a heated debate between teachers in the staff room can inspire you with new and creative teaching ideas. The outside, then, is where the real teaching opportunities are to be found. These are some of the things that "teaching from the outside in" means to us. If you are going to be a good teacher, you need to figure out why some things work and some things don't. You also need to be awake to the world around you, embracing practical, everyday moments as creative opportunities for teaching. Second, we previously wrote a very successful book titled *Teaching from the Inside Out* and we want to be sure that readers know that this book is intended as a companion piece to it. *Teaching from the Inside Out* is a book you can read; *Teaching from the Outside In* is a book you can use. The philosophies are the same, but the focus differs.

CHAPTER I

PLANNING PROFESSIONALLY

INTRODUCTION

PLANNING IS COMPLEX. It involves making decisions, predicting, guessing, visualizing, and restructuring. When teachers plan to teach, they make hundreds of small decisions. None of which individually may be life-changing, but together they add up to a final lesson plan that, hopefully, works. Throughout this book, we will use the word "works" a great deal. To us, and to most teachers, when something "works" it simply means that what we do accomplishes the goals we want to achieve or, at times, reaches goals even greater than those for which we planned.

WHY PLAN?

WRITTEN PLANNING happens when teachers brainstorm, organize, create, focus, and connect ideas into a coherent whole. Written plans help jog teachers' memories, give them a starting point, and help them organize an itinerary of things they want to accomplish during a class. Written lesson plans are also valuable because they give teachers a sense of security and confidence. They help teachers provide direction, structure, and focus. Plans also provide a written record of a given group's accomplishments. And plans give you accountability. Consider that at any given moment your administrator may ask you for a classroom itinerary. Being able to provide your principal with a written copy of your lesson or unit plan will save you much grief and embarrassment.

Something to Think About

Generally we like working with school-based cooperating teachers, but one of the things that annoys us about teachers is their loud, almost brazen claim that they do not use lesson plans. They're stretching the truth, of course. No good teacher goes into a class without knowing what is probably going to happen and planning for a variety of possible interventions with students.

Our student teachers are surprised when they talk with their cooperating teachers and hear, "I don't make lesson plans." And these experienced teachers really mean it; but, then again, they don't. Here's what we mean. These teachers, and they are some of the best, may not write lesson plans. But they do make lesson plans. No good teacher we know would dare enter a classroom without some systematic plan of action. If teachers entered a classroom cold, the students would eat them up!

Teachers who don't write plans still use them. One way to find out more about planning is to talk with a small number of experienced teachers about their planning. How do they do it? How has it changed over the years? Which type of plans work best in the heat of the classroom? They will be able to tell you a lot about the art and craft of writing lesson plans. You would be wise to listen.

There's also another reason to write lesson plans. This reason is obvious to us, but few teachers we know think about it. As experienced teachers, one thing we know about our vocation is that teaching is much less sociable than most people think. We also think that the teachers we know work too hard. Why write your lesson plans? Because written plans provide a clear way to communicate with other teachers, both substitutes and colleagues. If you are smart — and we think that to be a successful teacher you have to be smart — you will make some teacher friends and you will trade lesson plans. It makes life more social and much easier. Trust us. Don't be one of those teachers who hoards lesson plans or teaching ideas.

GOOD PLANNING

A GOOD LESSON PLAN is based on understanding four things: (1) the interests and abilities of your students, (2) your own interests and strengths, (3) your own beliefs about teaching and learning, and (4) your own openness to change your plans.

We know that initially it is difficult to construct a lesson or unit plan at the beginning of the school year simply because you have not met your students. We suggest that at this point, you plan your curriculum content and timing; however, only tentatively plan your "how-to-teach-this" (your methodology) until you have met and had an opportunity to watch your students. We say this because the interests and abilities of your students are paramount to a good lesson plan. Get to know them. Watch them and listen to what they have to say and before long, your teaching mind will begin to create lesson plans that will complement your unique group of learners.

Your own interests and strengths are imperative to good planning. Maybe you personally find the study of economic development in Japan uninteresting. We think this is a great opportunity for you to find ways in which to make it interesting for yourself. If you can turn your own disenchantment with a subject around, then certainly you can make it interesting for your students. Consider, too, your personal and professional strengths as a teacher. Are you a passionate and dramatic person? If so, incorporate this energy into your plans.

Clearly, your own beliefs about teaching and learning will influence your lesson plans. If you are a strong advocate of discovery learning, then your lesson plans will leave space for the students to discover and construct their own meaning. Likewise, if you believe more in reception learning or direct instruction, your plans will focus more on you as teacher finding, organizing and presenting information for your students. When presenting a lesson, you must make decisions about where to position yourself in the class and how to interact with students. You must also decide what "works" in your class. Will cooperative learning strategies work in a particular class, or are workshops, mini-lessons, lectures, or other structures more suitable in promoting learning? The answers differ, depending on your own beliefs and on the particular class you are teaching, or the particular time of day, or what happened yesterday.

All of this, we believe, is part of good planning. But your own openness and willingness to change your plans at any one moment, we think, is core to good planning. Don't let anyone tell you that teaching is easy. You have many choices to make. Sometimes what works once won't work again. Sometimes what looks like a beautifully crafted and interesting plan on paper flops when put into motion. Be open to this, and be ready at a moment's notice to change your plan. Unless you are a natural teacher, and there are few of them, it will take a long time to figure things out. Wise choices come from the labor of experience, and openness to things around you brings forth abundant opportunities.

As you grow into a competent, "good" teacher, be ready to be consumed by the job. If your experience is similar to ours, you will soon change from a person who says, consciously, "Now I am going to plan" to a person who is always planning. As you become a more flexible and accomplished teacher, your planning will also become more flexible and accomplished. Good planning allows for flexibility and adaptation.

Planning is an ongoing process that good teachers, fortunately or unfortunately, cannot turn off. Similar to the pilot light of a furnace, always ready to explode into flame, good teachers plan continually — always ready to explode into action. They plan informally while traveling to or from work, watching TV, or talking to friends. Some even keep a pad and pen on their night stand to jot down ideas that might come to them while they are sleeping. Teachers plan formally during weekends, evenings, and professional development sessions. Sometimes their planning is practical; sometimes it is theoretical. Most times, however, both practical and theoretical knowledge, combined with experience, are important. Experience forces you to grow and change constantly. If planning is difficult for you, as it is for most teachers, don't worry too much. Work hard and remember that, with experience, planning becomes natural, intuitive, and almost second nature. Soon, you too will be telling inexperienced student teachers "I don't make lesson plans anymore." And you will probably even believe it. But of course, similar to the teachers we know, you will still be planning.

WHERE DO WE START WHEN WE SIT DOWN TO PLAN?

WE BELIEVE THAT TEACHERS have to earn the right to be heard. Teachers who expect that students will listen to them just because they have been hired as a teacher will soon be shocked into reality. Students have little respect for position. You have to earn your respect. You have to be interesting enough to listen to. That's why, in this book, we have started with methodologies and teaching ideas instead of with content. We know, from the experience of falling on our faces over and over again, that content by itself is boring. You have chosen to teach

A Typical Plan Includes:

1. a title
2. goals and objectives (intents of lesson)
3. materials and resources
4. sequence of activities (time frame) with notes about how to attain outcomes
5. evaluation schemes (measurements/gauges of achievement)

social studies, or math, or accounting, or language arts because you love the content. But don't expect your students to share this love. Most of them are in your class because they have to be there, not because they want to. They are expecting to be bored. Your task is to engage them with your enthusiasm. Boring students is one of the most deadly mistakes a teacher can commit. It's a mistake, along with a lack of fairness, that students simply will not tolerate. Don't make that mistake!

When planning lessons, we often begin with an activity or a learning opportunity that we think our students will enjoy and that will support the important concepts and the content they need to learn. From this activity-based starting point we then make other decisions. (1) Which methodology should be used? (2) Will this methodology work with the concept to be taught? (3) How effective will this lesson be and when it has been completed, how effective has it been?

Already, numbering the actions we take when planning is probably giving you the wrong impression about planning. Planning is not linear. It doesn't happen 1, 2, 3. Planning is like making a tossed salad. The order in which the ingredients are added is not crucial; everything is there together. Other than starting with the first consideration of learning activity (and often we don't even do that, it's just a good rule of thumb), the activities of planning all happen together. However, like any other set of directions, it is easier to write about things as if they were completed in a step-by-step manner. But remember, things don't always happen like they are described.

Teachers' plans reflect their beliefs and values. These plans are also closely linked to the management strategies and routines that teachers choose to institute into their classes and the methods they use to evaluate their students. Traditional planning, management, and evaluation methods suggest strong teacher control; alternative approaches such as workshops and collaborative learning suggest classrooms where students are encouraged to become actively involved in their learning.

An important consideration when planning lessons is understanding where you are coming from as a teacher. We know that our beliefs and values as teachers, as well as our own personal strengths and interests, influence the choices we make in planning. Once we have worked to create interesting activities for our students, we need to consider what we want our students to learn — most textbooks about teaching call these things the learning outcomes. And although we find the term "outcomes" a bit mechanical, the word does make an important point. Teachers must be concerned about what their students learn. For example, we hope students will grow in academic maturity, will achieve the skills often called the 3Rs, and will achieve the curriculum requirements and objectives that are given in the government documents (in Canada, given by provincial ministries of education) that control how teachers must work. All these goals and objectives must become implicit in the content and activities of the lessons. These decisions then work together to direct further decisions about the way we organize and present the content of our lessons.

Goals and objectives specified by the teacher should include not only what the objectives are, but also why the lesson is important to the students' learning.

When writing goals and objectives for lesson plans, teachers should consider and note points about their students. *How do the intents of the lesson connect to the students' own interests and experiences?* Teachers should try to use active verbs that help them organize what the students are doing and construct evaluation ideas that help students understand if they have achieved the objectives or stated outcomes of the lesson plan and the course. And, if appropriate, teachers should clearly identify the degree of proficiency expected.

Teachers may wish to consider sharing their planning process with their students. Although not commonly done, there are many reasons to tell students what you are doing. First, from an ethical perspective, there is simply no reason not to tell students what is happening in class. The more they know and understand, the more they can become part of what is going on in the classroom. When students become an active part of the process, they no longer are the victims of someone who is doing things to them, they are now an active part of the team. Second, from a practical sense, sharing with students often contributes to the building of relationships between you and your students. Students who come to own their learning become better learners. Third, from an instructional sense, students can learn how to structure and organize their own ideas and work as they negotiate presentation methods, time, and assignments. In the jargon of education, they become more empowered. Understanding the planning process can help students to organize their learning and to understand expectations (assignments, evaluation methods) more clearly.

Here's a hint about lesson planning, and it's a hint that took some of us longer to learn than others — especially for those of us not naturally well-organized. Make a lesson plan once, and make it good the first time. When planning as a beginning teacher, this advice will seem oppressive. Planning well the first time will take a long time. But, as you become more experienced, planning will become more natural and take less time. While it may seem that informal, mental planning is sufficient, written, well-organized and carefully thought-out lessons result in making learning and teaching easier — especially over the long haul. Almost everyone can make a lesson plan one night and remember it the very next morning, but that next morning will not be the last morning of your teaching career. There is always next year, and the year after. Write your lesson plans with the coming years in mind. Also, after the lesson, go back and write down a few notes about what worked and what parts of the lesson might be improved on. Then, find an organized way to keep your plans from one year to the next. Make this organization something you can live with and something that is easy for you.

CONSIDERING THE CURRICULUM

WE HAVE TALKED much about methods, but we also need to note that every lesson plan is about something. A lesson plan has a content, usually called a curriculum. Lesson plans must always consider the official curriculum. As a way

Finding Examples of Units

Most teachers organize and teach from unit plans. See if you can find some sample unit plans that teachers have made. (These might be professionally done, such as teachers' guides to textbooks, or school-based units that a subject area has put together as a team.) When you have collected samples of these units, study them for content, methods, format, and design. From what you have seen, can you choose a tentative pattern that seems most useful for you?

ACTIVITY:

Observe a 45 minute lesson, noting all the transitions used by the teacher (transitions provide a clue as to how many different activities have been included in the lesson.) Make a list of the transitions you observed, and then add to the list from your own knowledge and ideas.

to begin planning, let the program of studies (often the official name for the prescribed curriculum you are required to teach) guide the lessons you choose to teach.

There are two reasons for knowing the official curriculum. First, it is the legal responsibility of your profession. You are required by law to teach the curriculum. Second, the official curriculum offers practical ideas. In most mandated programs of studies, the official lists of knowledge, skills, and attitudes sections are, in themselves, rich hints for creating lesson plans. Take a look at the program of studies, and especially look at the verbs. Try to design activities that mimic the objectives of the curriculum.

For example, a typical skill objective in your program of studies may say "Students will be able to explore a variety of resources about the same topic and evaluate these resources for bias." Many people would see this as an outcome statement; however, it is also a lesson plan idea. The program of studies is suggesting that, as a teacher, some of your tasks are to provide your students with a variety of resources on a specific topic, to create (or better yet have your students create) an evaluation instrument that includes a test for bias, and to help your students learn how to use the instrument that has been created. So, do it. It might take a little time to complete these tasks — finding the materials on the same topic and creating the evaluation instrument — but if you take the time to do it properly this year, next year is a breeze.

The curriculum guide can also help in creating long range and unit plans. It will largely determine the length and number of units to include in a year, and will outline key concepts and objectives to focus on with the students. The challenge in creating year plans and unit plans is to create balanced, manageable units of study that reflect the needs of the students, your own interests and strengths, and the mandate of the curriculum. But, similar to all planning, these are little problems that can be overcome by just working at them. Our advice is to do just that — work at them. That's where we think our advice about making other teacher friends is so helpful. You might as well make the work a social time. If you are a good teacher, you are going to have to plan. You might as well have fun in the process.

OTHER PLANNING CONSIDERATIONS

THERE ARE A NUMBER of other things that teachers should consider when creating lesson and unit plans. For example, timing is a key point. A principle we follow is never to give enough time for students to be finished. It is easier to extend time and appear kind than to cut down time and look mean. Dead space can be a killer. Provide smooth and effective transitions. Transitions help students connect one activity to another; they are also valuable in effective management in the classroom.

As we mentioned before, earning the right to be heard is a key to teaching. Research repeatedly suggests two points: (1) students want to like their teachers and (2) students want to learn. We encourage teachers not to be hesitant to expect hard work from students. If they like you, they will usually try to please you. A common mistake teachers make is to believe that students will like them if they squander gifts and charity (something for nothing) on them. But we believe that constantly receiving something for nothing both erodes the self-motivation and the soul of anyone.

Student projects are a key to effective planning. Projects give students some time to rally around and foster group identity. When students work hard on a project and complete it, they usually feel good when it's done. We also encourage teachers not to be afraid to involve the affective in teaching.

Finally, another belief we hold is that all education has a political agenda. Knowledge is worth knowing if it improves the world. We encourage you to ask how what you are doing in your planning helps to improve the world. On the surface, such a comment may seem less than rigorous; however, if teaching has no promise or hope for the future, then why do it?

Observe a lesson given by a teacher. Each time the teacher begins a new lesson segment, record the time the segment begins and the type of activity that occurs during that segment. Some examples of activities are "showing a film," "reviewing concepts," "giving a test," "lecturing," and "conducting a discussion." Try to observe and record the teacher's transition statements and actions as well as the lesson segments. After completing the observation, consider the amount of time that was spent on each type of activity. Make some general observations about the nature of the classes you observe. What kind of balance did you observe? How well did it work? What types of transitions were effective? Use a chart as follows:

Time	Activity	Transition Statement/Action

SAMPLE PLANNING STRATEGIES

THE FOLLOWING INCIDENTS deal with planning and were recalled by student teachers immediately after their student teaching experiences. Read and respond to each of the strategies, and then provide your own, based on your teaching experiences and observations.

STRATEGY 1. During the first week of my student teaching experience I received a teacher's planning book which turned out to be invaluable to me. My first week of teaching allowed me to get a good grasp of where the students were and where we were going. So I wrote lessons in the planning book for the next four weeks. This gave me a guideline to follow and was very useful. Before teaching each class I felt the most essential thing was being very familiar with the material I was teaching, so I reviewed at night and each morning, writing down important points and making a type of "schedule" to follow.

Observing a Peer Teaching Presentation

This observation exercise can be used to observe a peer teaching in a presentation style. It can also be used to assess a lesson you have taught and videotaped. Viewing and assessing your own teaching performances can help you become a better teacher. Consider the following teacher behaviours, and consider which of them you or your colleague managed effectively, and which need more practice.

1. How appropriate was the content of the lesson? How do you know?
2. How prepared was the teacher overall?
3. How well did the teacher — explain goals and purposes? examples and transitions? display enthusiasm for the lesson? display enthusiasm for the students? extend and strengthen student thinking?
4. What do you think went best about the way the lesson was planned and organized?
5. What could be improved?
6. What were the most effective aspects of the lesson presentation?
7. What could be improved?
8. If you had been a student in this class, how would you have felt about the teacher's interaction with you?

STRATEGY 2. I first consulted the TRM (Teacher Resource Manual), the curriculum guide, the teacher material available, the unit plan, the library resource, and video resources. I then used a photocopied sheet that looked as follows:

Objectives:

Procedures:

Materials:

Curriculum Mandates fulfilled:

Planning usually took me an hour for each class hour. I had to think through my classes comprehensively before teaching them. My planning paid off. I planned extensively on the weekend for the entire week, and merely brushed up during prep periods. Prep periods were generally devoted to marking.

STRATEGY 3. In planning, I tried to aim for:

- diversity (a variety of activities)
- options (can do either this or this)
- active participation (getting as many people involved in some way as possible)
- strong opening, one that was fun, made sense and provided "set"

I did much thinking in the evening but I found it useful to get up in the morning and write my lesson plans out then as opposed to the night before. This was my "set" for the day — getting all the things I had to do into my head.

I didn't meet my aims all the time, because I found it difficult to constantly re-invent things every night. I tried to plan as I went along, adjusting and altering things in mid-stream to better fit the unique circumstances of that particular week. I think this was a good idea, but it was very difficult and very exhausting.

STRATEGY 4. I generally planned for a week at a time in advance, over the weekend. These plans were mere outlines that were to serve as guidelines for what I wanted to accomplish throughout the week.

Then, each night (or sometimes during student work time and at noon hours) I would make more detailed plans for the classes to be taught the next day using the week's plans as reference.

I tried to take many factors into account such as the day of the week, extra-curricular activities, and previous class schedules. I tried to mix up my lessons over the course of a week. One day — group activity. Another day — notes and lecture for some of the time. Another day — individual work.

STRATEGY 5. I first set goals, both long and short term. I had specific culminating activities in mind, and kept in mind how the students performed for me. The classroom atmosphere played an important factor, as well as outside activities (i.e. school dances, staff meetings, etc.) I tried to break down the lesson into smaller pieces, and considered student learning levels.

STRATEGY 6. I tried to plan a week at a time. While some days we would sail through my planned lesson, other days an unintended aside would lead us away from my original objectives. At first this scared me because I felt like I was losing the control I needed to maintain as the teacher. I never thought I would be at all breezy in my lesson planning, but I began discovering that the best moments in my classroom, the ones where I thought that I saw real learning, happened spontaneously. I decided that while I always had to come to class with a plan, I had to be equally prepared to change that plan at a moment's notice. Looking back now, I realize that the more confident I felt in front of my students, the more open and willing I became to seize the sudden teaching opportunities presented to me daily, sometimes hourly.

PLANNING LESSONS

LESSON PLANNING is an important, and often understated, part of teaching. Because every teacher makes some sort of lesson plan, often planning is taken for granted. But planning is not as easy as it sometimes seems. When making a lesson plan — especially one that "works" — there are many things to consider. Even though you are not an experienced teacher, you probably have a good sense of what is needed in a solid lesson plan. Take a moment now to jot down all of the things you think are needed in an effective lesson plan. Some of your planning considerations may have included the following:

- What are the main objectives?
- What materials are needed?
- How much time do I have available for this lesson?
- How will I introduce the lesson and provide motivation for the students?
- What is it necessary to recall or review from previous lessons?
- How should the lesson unfold; what are the parts of the lesson?
- What opportunities will be provided for questioning and demonstrating?
- How will students be actively participating?
- What forms of evaluation will be used to assess student learning?
- How will the students follow up this learning?
- How will I conclude this lesson?

Lesson Plan Format

I. Goals/Objectives/Intents (why is it important to teach this lesson)

II. Materials: (List materials needed to complete the plan — what reminders to you need? Are there any particular difficulties that must be considered?)

III. Activities: (what are the strategies used to help students reach the goals and objectives set out)
(note: timing should be considered along with the activities)
1. Beginning the class
   a. Review of last day's class
   b. Introduction to today's class
2. (Activity Steps in the Body of Plan)
3. Wrap-up (summarizing key points the students will take away with them, be able to apply to the next lessons)
   a. "Closure"
   b. key idea to remember from the lesson
   c. Assignment
   d. Evaluation of Plan
   e. Alternative Plan

IV. Self-evaluation: How did the plan go? Should you do it again? What should you change?

COMPONENTS OF A LESSON PLAN

GET WITH A GROUP of colleagues and arrive at a consensus for the necessary components and order of an effective lesson plan. You will probably arrive at a format that has some similarities to the one on the right.

Planning for teaching can seem like a never-ending task. When we first think about planning, it might seem like staring out over an endless ocean. But planning can become much easier when we begin by considering several key components. We suggest that keeping your focus small and simple will help you make some sense of planning.

There is no **one** way to plan a lesson or one format that is superior to all others. Considering, as you have above, the important elements of a lesson plan, you can choose to organize your plan in a variety of ways. Three examples are offered here for you to try out. We suggest that you create a lesson plan using each of the suggested formats, and then self-evaluate with the questions that follow.

LESSON PLANNING FORMATS

1. IDAE MODEL

The IDAE model of lesson planning was first proposed by Ted Aoki. It is intended to be holistic rather than linear. The Aoki model has no identifiable beginning or end. The components of the IDAE model are defined as follows:

INTENTS (I) are expressions of interests, desired goals or possibilities. They may be explicit written objectives or implicit desires, or interests of individuals.

DISPLAYS (D) are instructional or learning materials which are typically displayed, materials with which students and teachers interact in an instructional setting. Displays can be pictures, written materials, spoken words, maps, etc.

ACTIVITIES (A) refer to teacher and/or student activities defined together with "intents" and "displays." Class activities may be predefined by teachers or may occur in interactional situations.

EVALUATION (E) is an activity which occurs with the first step in lesson development. In fact, lesson evaluation and lesson development can be seen as two aspects of the same inquiry. It is useful to think of (1) "Taken-for-granted" evaluation (evaluation done without consciousness of the evaluative act), (2) "In-process" evaluation (formative evaluation), (3) "After-the-fact" evaluation (summative evaluation). They suggest possible modes of evaluation as well as the timing of the evaluation activity.

One way of making sense of instructional programs is to acknowledge the guiding principle of multiple perspectives. The same phenomena can be viewed very differently by different people. Consider for a moment how the same sunrise could be seen by a person who has to go to work very early, a youngster who is going fishing early in the morning, or a prisoner who is scheduled to be executed in the morning.

The notion of perspective when trying to make sense of instructional lessons is crucial. It allows us to entertain the following about lessons: (1) that underlying any lesson is a perspective; (2) that developing intents, designing displays, teacher/student activities, or evaluating are perspective-guided activities; (3) that the kind of interest, the form of knowledge, the mode of teaching, the way of learning, the modality of evaluation, etc., embodied in a program reflect the underlying guiding perspective.

Perspective is "a mode of seeing, in that extended sense of 'see' in which it means to discern, apprehend, understand or grasp. It is a particular way of looking at life, a particular manner of construing the world, as when we speak of a historical perspective, scientific perspective, an esoteric perspective, a common-sense perspective, or even the bizarre perspectives embodied in dreams or in hallucinations." (Geertz, in Werner, W. (1977). A study of perspective in social studies. An unpublished dissertation, University of Alberta, Edmonton, Alberta, p. 29) Understanding perspective provides us with an underlying rationale for our actions in that it provides us with a justification for acting the way we do.

I - Intents
D - Displays
A - Activities
E - Evaluation

PROGRAM

E

A

I

D

Perspective 1

Perspective 2

Perspective 3

2. LINEAR LESSON PLAN

Teacher Activities	Student Activities

CLOSURE/ASSIGNMENTS:

Date_____

Unit_____

Lesson Plan_____

Class_____

Topic_____

Time Available_____

Objectives _____

_____

_____

_____

Materials/Resources _____

_____

_____

_____

3. HUNTER'S TEACHING MODEL

Hunter's Teaching Model was designed by Madeline Hunter [see Hunter, Madeline. (1990). *Discipline that develops self-discipline: a programmed book.* El Segundo, CA: TIP Publications], an education researcher, teacher and principal who spent a lot of time trying to identify a lesson format that was most effective for student learning. Although Madeline Hunter's work is sometimes controversial, we think this lesson plan example, quoted from her work, can be helpful.

Written By:	
Grade:	
Time:	**Date:**
Subject:	**Topic:**
Objective and Purpose anticipated outcome of the lesson	• what they are learning • why the lesson is important/why they are doing it • what they will be expected to be able to do at the end of the lesson
Anticipatory Set	• establishing lesson's rationale and motivation • link to students' past experience or knowledge • actively involves learner • relevant to the objective of the upcoming lesson
Materials	
Input	• concepts and skill to be explained or developed • relevant, questions, information, activities
Modeling	• demonstration or showing of concepts or skills • examples, illustrations, simulations, models or demonstrations
Guided Practice	• in-class practice of concepts and skills with teacher guidance • provide feedback
Independent Practice	• practice concepts and skills without teacher guidance (could be homework)
Closure	• re-focus students on the essential elements of what they have learned
Evaluation	• formal or informal checking for understanding

FOLLOW-UP QUESTIONS

1. How does this type of plan cause me to think in different ways?
2. How might this planning format change the way I teach? The way I think about my students?
3. Are there drawbacks to this type of planning approach?
4. What will the students be doing when I am teaching?
5. Does this lesson follow or precede a very active or exciting one? How will I help the students re-focus or concentrate?
6. How can I connect this lesson to other content areas, real-life experiences, or future tasks or activities?
7. What considerations come to mind as I "mentally rehearse" the lesson?
8. Can I keep control of the situation that I create by using the activities in this lesson plan?
9. What do my students like to do?
10. What have we done before? Should we consider new activities?
11. What, from my experience, won't work? Is this class any different than other classes I have taught before?
12. What are the personalities of the specific people in this group? And, so what? How will these personalities affect what goes on in class? What should I be careful to avoid, or to do?
13. Are there any students who have missed a portion of previous lessons? What responsibilities will I take and what will I place on them?
14. Do I need to make any accommodations for a particular child or group? Have I considered a range of learning styles?
15. What do I like/enjoy doing personally? What best fits my own personality?
16. What do I believe about teaching students? (For example, do I believe that self-esteem is important? Do I believe in encouraging success? Do I want to encourage activities or quietness? Do I think this group needs especially good directions, bite-size pieces, etc.?)

ACTIVE AND INTERACTIVE LESSONS

GOOD LESSONS should be both active and interactive. Students learn best when they are involved in their learning and when they are stimulated, not bored. Questions, effectively introduced in a lesson, can help stimulate interest and thought. Some of the many purposes for asking questions, and encouraging students to ask questions, include:

1. to arouse interest and curiosity
2. to focus attention on an issue
3. to stimulate learners to ask questions
4. to diagnose specific learning difficulties
5. to encourage reflection and self-evaluation
6. to review content previously learned

ACTIVITY:

Review a unit or lesson plan that you have developed. From the anecdotal and evaluative comments that you included after teaching the lesson or unit, and from the suggestions given to you by your cooperating teacher or other observers of your lesson, rewrite your plan and incorporate these suggestions and ideas in order to be able to teach a more effective lesson next time.

7. to teach through student answers
8. to probe deeper
9. to redirect or structure the flow of ideas
10. to allow expressions of feelings
11. to manage or remind students of a procedure in the class
12. to diagnose specific learning difficulties

Most reasons for asking questions can be categorized as follows:
1. interest and attention-getting
2. diagnosing and checking
3. recalling specific facts or information
4. management concerns
5. encouraging higher level thinking processes
6. structuring and redirecting learning
7. allowing expressions of opinions and personal reactions

Many questions shape or set up the learners' responses. Well-formulated questions can serve as advanced organizers, providing the framework into which must be placed the response which will follow.

PLANNING SUGGESTIONS

WE THINK THE FOLLOWING suggestions will help you make good instructional plans, but not tie yourself to your plans so that you cannot be sensitive to anything else that might happen.

1. Remember that a key question in lesson planning is "What do you *really* want to do and why is it important?" There are always at least two things being taught during a given lesson — the content you choose and the way you choose to teach it. Ask and answer the questions: What goals do you have for your class? What general principles do you want to follow when you teach? How do you think people learn? How do you think people should learn?

2. Review the form of your plan. Reread your plans, checking for things you don't understand. (If possible, find a critical friend who can tell you what can't be understood.) You will always remember what you wanted to do the next day, but if you are not careful or specific you may become an outsider to your own thinking next year.

3. Make your lesson plan easy to use "in front" of your class. Make sure you can follow your plan on the spot. Remember what you are doing. You have to be able to work in "traffic" in front of the group. You can't be looking down, having a hard time reading what you wrote.

4. We also try to remember and use two important principles. They are: (1) *Students want to learn; they just don't want to be bored.* (2) *Students have an unique sense of fair play. They don't want to be manipulated.*

We think there are three ways to help make your lesson plans easy to use in your classroom. First, use good spacing. Put some room between the directions to yourself. Second, use numbers instead of dashes or even letters of the alphabet. Numbers are easier to follow than letters. Third, use colored highlighters. These can help draw attention to the key points in your plan. Remember not to highlight everything. Many different colors are pretty, but they can become confusing when trying to read your work quickly in front of a class.

HOW TO BEGIN UNIT PLANNING

HERE ARE SOME OF OUR SUGGESTIONS for beginning your planning.

- Consider your goals, objectives, or anticipated student outcomes, and think about how you can best help your students achieve these ends.
- Decide how long the unit should take in the yearly scheme of things.
- Find or make a big calendar that shows the days. (You will need enough room to write in the spaces for each day.) You can find these calendars almost anywhere. Banks and drug stores often provide them for free. Or you can make your own. They don't have to be too slick.
- Rough in all the activities (formal evaluations, research days, reviews, movies or media, and tried-and-true lesson ideas).
- Look for special considerations of the school calendar that might disrupt your plans such as holidays, school report cards, or meet the teacher days — change things now to reflect these days.

A FINAL WORD

ALTHOUGH WE MADE THIS POINT earlier, we believe it is worth repeating. As a beginning teacher you will meet many experienced teachers who take great pride in claiming that they no longer plan. Don't be deceived. These teachers are getting by on experience and the fact that they have presented a particular lesson or activity many times before. Only practice allows the experienced teacher to get through a class without a lesson plan. New teachers do not often have the experience to improvise and fly by the seat of their pants. They need to plan.

All good teachers know what they are going to do when they enter a classroom. Without a lesson plan you would have to rely on luck for good things to happen. You know you need a lesson if you are to teach. However, planning a lesson is not the end of teaching. Good teachers are not constrained by lesson plans. The classroom is dynamic. Wise teachers are sensitive to the possibility that new things can happen. Teachable moments are not to be squandered.

CHAPTER 2

EVALUATION

INTRODUCTION

EVALUATION IS AN INTEGRAL PART of our school system, indeed our society. There is no way to avoid evaluation: it is part of almost everything we do. We evaluate people when we first meet them (first impressions) and every time we see them thereafter. We evaluate the ideas we meet, either including them in our existing framework of beliefs or dismissing them. We evaluate situations, opportunities, and values.

To many teachers and almost every student, evaluation is an unsettling concept. And, for some of us, evaluation is a real fear. We have bad memories of it; we have been hurt. But evaluation need not be harmful; indeed it can be a very positive force in our educational system if fairly and honestly applied.

An important aspect of any evaluation is the criteria used when making an evaluation. Sometimes the criteria are explicit and easy to apply; at other times they are implicit and evaluation becomes messy and unclear. An important part of being a good teacher is to make evaluation criteria as explicit and understandable as possible to students. Another important aspect of teaching is to help students themselves become effective evaluators. By encouraging self-evaluation we can offer students a sense of investment and responsibility in their own education.

Evaluation is part of everything we do, and should be seen in connection with ourselves as well as our students. How often do we take time to evaluate our own teaching performances, ideas, and lesson strategies? Are we able to assess ourselves as well as our students? If the answer is no, we might benefit from some help. Inviting a colleague to observe our teaching can be a very valuable experience. It can be valuable to have a videotape made of our teaching so that we can watch ourselves.

Take the opportunity to observe a colleague or have a colleague observe you. What types of observations did you make? Ask yourself or your colleague the following questions:

Did I fidget? Did I seem relaxed? If I seemed nervous or distracted, what was the cause? Did I make eye contact with the speaker/listener? Did I interrupt when someone else was speaking? What sorts of non-verbal cues did I use? Did I use my body movements to emphasize points?

How could I change ineffective or distracting behaviours and actions? What can I do to replace these behaviours? Where can I get practice and further feedback about my teaching performances?

EVALUATION OF STUDENT PERFORMANCES

WE BELIEVE THAT many evaluation practices that go on in schools today are offensive. We, as teachers, are more thoughtless about evaluation than about any other area of our work. We simply don't think about what we do. And we're not just pointing our fingers at others. We too, the authors of this book, did not always use tests and other evaluations as well as we could or should have. We hope that this book helps correct some of the mistakes we, and others, have made.

Over the course of a school year, teachers use a repertoire of evaluation methods to meet a variety of objectives. However, the conventional evidence teachers use to find out that learning has occurred does not always coincide with what an individual student has actually learned. In other words, we sometimes test unimportant things that students haven't learned and don't test important things that they have learned. Why? Because some things are easier to test than others and we have a tendency to test the easiest, not the most crucial.

Often our evaluation tools seem scientific because they assess specific, quantifiable skills. However, what's tested may be very superficial. We need to change. If teachers are really going to make evaluation useful and important, they need to go beyond traditional practices of assessment and evaluation. They need to develop evaluations that will generate more comprehensive and realistic findings and uncover more significant understandings about how their students learn.

Our evaluative practices are often an indication of the teaching methods we choose. They are part of the curriculum we teach; they are not "extra" to our curriculum — attached to the end. If our evaluations are unfair, or mean, or abstract, or excessively factual, then our teaching is unfair, mean, abstract, and excessively factual. Because evaluation is so important, it must be done thoughtfully. We need to question the validity of traditional paper and pencil learning measures. And we need to continually remind ourselves of the purposes of our evaluation.

Why are we evaluating students? There are several reasons, most of them legitimate. We cannot assess everything students know or can do, but we can use a variety of **diagnostic** evaluation strategies and tools to determine our students' levels of knowledge and understanding, to identify their strengths and weaknesses, and (a key) to improve their learning. We can evaluate to provide informative **feedback** to students and ourselves, an interactive and recursive process that can help us assess the effectiveness of a particular instructional strategy.

Evaluation can be used to ensure that students are accountable for their learning and performance. It can **motivate** them to produce the best work they are capable of producing. This type of **summative** evaluation (oral reports, quizzes, presentations, activities) focuses student attention on what is important for their success in a given class and in their lives. As teachers, we must never forget that students will come to believe that what we evaluate is the most important part of their education. A final type of evaluation, **recording and reporting**, serves to inform students and their parents about overall achievement and progress, and to make decisions about placement, grouping, and promotion.

DILEMMAS OF EVALUATION

NO EVALUATION IS ENTIRELY OBJECTIVE or fair to every student. Yet, as teachers, we want to be fair to all students. The gap between our desire and our reality pushes us to ask these difficult questions: How can we evaluate our students fairly and honestly? What should we be evaluating in our students' performances?

There are many cases in teaching, similar to other professions, where our desires do not match up with our realities. For example, formal evaluation situations such as testing are often used to motivate students to perform to the best of their ability, and yet we do not want to give students the message that the only reason for completing an assignment or studying for a test is to get a good grade. We need to find balances between external motivations and those that are more intrinsic. What is fair and productive to evaluate? Should we look only at the product and performance of the students, or should our evaluation strategies also consider the process, attitude, oral skills, effort, and participation of the students? The whole question of evaluation is murky, at best. Perhaps, just by asking the questions out loud, we are already beginning to consider these elements without being aware or it. If we believe it is important to assess attitude and effort, what strategies might be used to consider these aspects of the students' work?

The following are evaluation guidelines from the *Principles of Fair Student Assessment Practices for Education in Canada* (1993), which was developed by a working group guided by a joint advisory committee. We hope you will consider these guidelines when creating your own evaluation methods.

I. **Developing and Choosing Methods for Assessment**
    1. Assessment methods should be developed or chosen so that inferences drawn about the knowledge, skills, attitudes, and behaviors possessed by each student are valid and not open to misinterpretation.
    2. Assessment methods should be clearly related to the goals and objectives of instruction and be compatible with the instructional approaches used.
    3. When developing or choosing assessment methods, consideration should be given to the consequences of the decisions to be made in light of the obtained information.
    4. More than one assessment method should be used to ensure comprehensive and consistent indications of student performance.
    5. Assessment methods should be suited to the backgrounds and prior experiences of students.
    6. Content and language that would generally be viewed as sensitive, sexist, or offensive should be avoided.
    7. Assessment instruments translated into a second language or transferred from another context or location should be accompanied by evidence that inferences based on these instruments are valid for the intended purpose.

II. Collecting Assessment Information

1. Students should be told why assessment information is being collected and how this information will be used.
2. An assessment procedure should be used under conditions suitable to its purpose and form.
3. In assessments involving observations, checklists, or rating scales, the number of characteristics to be assessed at one time should be small enough and concretely described so that the observations can be made accurately.
4. The directions provided to students should be clear, complete, and appropriate for the ability, age, and grade level of the students.
5. In assessments involving selection items (e.g., true-false, multiple-choice), the directions should encourage students to answer all items without threat of penalty.
6. When collecting assessment information, interactions with students should be appropriate and consistent.
7. Unanticipated circumstances that interfere with the collection of assessment information should be noted and recorded.
8. A written policy should guide decisions about the use of alternate procedures for collecting assessment information from students with special needs and students whose proficiency in the language of instruction is inadequate for them to respond in the anticipated manner.

III. Judging and Scoring Student Performance

1. Before an assessment method is used, a procedure for scoring should be prepared to guide the process of judging the quality of a performance or product, the appropriateness of an attitude or behavior, or the correctness of an answer.
2. Before an assessment method is used, students should be told how their responses or the information they provide will be judged or scored.
3. Care should be taken to ensure that results are not influenced by factors that are not relevant to the purpose of the assessment.
4. Comments formed as part of scoring should be based on the response made by the students and presented in a way that students can understand and use them.
5. Any changes made during scoring should be based upon a demonstrated problem with the initial scoring procedure. The modified procedure should then be used to rescore all previously scored responses.
6. An appeal process should be described to students at the beginning of each school year or course of instruction that they may use to appeal a result.

IV. Summarizing and Interpreting Results

1. Procedures for summarizing and interpreting results for a reporting period should be guided by a written policy.

2. The way in which summary comments and grades are formulated and interpreted should be explained to students and their parents/guardians.

3. The individual results used and the process followed in deriving summary comments and grades should be described in sufficient detail so that the meaning of a summary comment or grade is clear.

4. Combining disparate kinds of results into a single summary should be done cautiously. To the extent possible, achievement, effort, participation, and other behaviors should be graded separately.

5. Summary comments and grades should be based on more than one assessment result so as to ensure adequate sampling of broadly defined learning outcomes.

6. The results used to produce summary comments and grades should be combined in a way that ensures that each result receives its intended emphasis or weight.

7. The basis for interpretation should be carefully described and justified.

8. Interpretations of assessment results should take into account the backgrounds and learning experiences of the students.

9. Assessment results that will be combined into summary comments and grades should be stored in a way that ensures their accuracy at the time they are summarized and interpreted.

10. Interpretations of assessment results should be made with due regard for limitations in the assessment methods used, problems encountered in collecting the information and judging or scoring it, and limitations in the basis used for interpretation.

STRATEGIES FOR EFFECTIVE EVALUATION

WE EVALUATE OUR STUDENTS and their work continually. Often evaluations can be unpleasant for students, who respond by going to many lengths to avoid being evaluated. They miss exams, either by not studying or by not even showing up to take them, proclaiming loudly that they don't care anyway, blaming the teacher for being ineffective or "stupid," and responding by not giving their best effort. We think they are immature or, worse yet, rebellious. They think they are independent or that they are "taking a stand." Whatever the excuse or reason, the result is often disastrous. Some students just haven't yet learned that there are some things in life you just put up with, like it or not. In our saner, or maybe crazier moments, we wonder if it's such a good thing that students who really do well in school are those who have learned to "put up with stuff." We remember our own experiences in school. One of the reasons we have succeeded in our profession is that we never openly rebelled against those things we knew were stupid at the time. We just kept quiet and endured. It makes you wonder: did we do the right thing or not?

Measures

diagnostic measures: used to diagnose learning difficulties during instruction

formative measures: used to monitor learning progress during instruction

summative measures: used to assess achievement at the end of instruction

Hopefully, teaching and evaluating can change. As teachers, we can provide experiences that help all students gain some type of **success** and enable them to show their strengths as well as their weaknesses. If we are to do that we should employ **a variety** of methods for evaluating student progress, use diagnostic processes as well as summative ones, encourage students to formulate their own questions as well as answering the teacher's questions, and provide a variety of open-ended opportunities for students to show their critical and creative abilities as well as their abilities to memorize and apply concepts.

Good evaluation is not a teacher power-play. Instead, evaluation should be a cooperative process that involves the active engagement of students and teachers. It should be a natural process, involving diagnostic, formative, and summative measures, rather than being seen as a frightening "event" in students' lives. Evaluation procedures should be seen as meaningful to the students as well as to the teachers and be an extension of learning for both.

Evaluation methods can encourage students to synthesize a variety of knowledge and process components, rather than seeing their learning in isolated segments. We can give students opportunities, both formally and informally, to demonstrate their understanding and ability to apply, formulate, create, and critically analyze. Although we need not follow the levels of Bloom's Taxonomy to the letter, they are a good guide for reminding ourselves to challenge students to higher levels of thinking rather than continually regurgitating material that they are unable to see as valuable.

We do know some things about student learning that should help us create better evaluations. We know, for example, that students learn best when they are positive and feel successful about themselves and their work. Rather than being embarrassed by their mistakes, they can be encouraged to learn from their mistakes and to identify their mistakes for themselves.

Understanding these points helps us respond as teachers. We think that it is helpful to be specific in your comments to students, to enable them to learn from their mistakes or their weaknesses. We know that we can provide encouragement to students by pointing out what they did well, as well as identifying one or two specific areas for improvement.

For example, it is better to write on a student's paper "By placing a thesis statement which gives the focus for your paper in the opening paragraph, you are helping anyone who reads your paper make sense of your points immediately." or "Punctuation always goes inside quotation marks." than it is to write "A weak introduction." or "Check punctuation rules."

In the former cases, students both are instructed in good writing and know how to respond specifically to your request. The result is simple: they do better work. Once students realize what they **can** do well, they often will be more enthusiastic about focusing on how they can improve in other areas.

BROOKFIELD'S "CHARACTERISTICS OF HELPFUL EVALUATION"

While Stephen Brookfield's characteristics of helpful evaluation are based on his study of adult learners, we believe they are relevant to learners of all ages [see Brookfield, Stephen D. (1990). The Skillful Teacher. San Francisco, CA: Jossey Bass].

Stephen Brookfield (1990) emphasizes the threat of evaluation to adults' fragile egos, and the responsibility of the evaluator to be sensitive to adult learners' feelings. He points out the tension between the relationship of trust that most facilitators work hard to establish with adult learners, and the critical final judgments of evaluation that can damage this trust. Ultimately, if learners are angry or hurt or made defensive by evaluation, they may not be able to deal with the evaluative information. Thus, progress is not enhanced when evaluation does not attend to learners' feelings.

Brookfield suggests that an evaluation process should have the following ten characteristics. These characteristics will ensure that the evaluation process is honest and helpful, while being as sensitive as possible to adult learner needs and the delicate learner-teacher relationship.

1. **Clarity:** Teachers must make criteria and methods for evaluation crystal-clear to learners, and use terms and language that people understand.

2. **Immediacy:** Teachers should make evaluation immediate. Learners look for feedback immediately after performing a skill and are able to remember and incorporate suggestions into their performance while the memory of the last trial is still fresh in their minds. The sooner evaluation occurs, the more helpful it will be.

3. **Regularity:** Teachers should incorporate evaluation as a regular part of instruction rather than save it for end-of-unit periods. When evaluation is more frequent, it becomes less threatening, and learners are less apt to be surprised by the results. More regular evaluation also delivers more information more immediately to learners, which maximizes its effect on improving learning.

4. **Accessibility:** Teachers should be as available as possible to learners during and after the evaluative information is delivered. Learners often want to seek clarification, respond to the feedback, discuss concerns, or sometimes just to get a little comfort.

5. **Individualized:** Teachers should personalize the detail but focus on the learners' actions. Help learners avoid interpreting the evaluative feedback as judgments about them personally.

6. **Affirming:** Teachers should acknowledge whatever learners have achieved before delivering the critical feedback. Critical feedback itself needs to be embedded in a basic attitude of respect for the learners' efforts towards accomplishing the task.

7. **Future-Oriented:** Teachers should provide clear and specific suggestions to learners about future actions they could take to improve their performance or understandings.

8. **Justifiable:** Teachers should show learners the reasons for the criticism, matching learner performance to the criteria required, as well as showing how criticisms spring from a basic concern for the students' learning and a desire to assist them in reaching their own goals.

9. **Educative:** Teachers need to ultimately remember their responsibilities to help learners learn. Comments that are warm and sympathetic may make learners feel better, but are they educative?

10. **Selective:** Teachers need to avoid overwhelming learners with too much evaluative information. Focus only on a few areas that learners can work on. Learners can't improve everything at once.

TYPES OF EVALUATION

TRADITIONAL AND AUTHENTIC ASSESSMENT DEFINED

Traditional Assessment generally refers to assessment whereby students are required to respond to questions by selecting or providing a short answer. In contrast, **authentic** or **performance assessment** is a form of evaluation that requires students to perform a task rather than select an answer from a ready-made test. Often the student engages in a task that resembles real-world or classroom activities.

Types of Traditional Assessment

1. **Multiple Choice:** identifying specific facts such as who, what, when and where
2. **Alternative Response (i.e., true/false):** identifying correctness of statement of facts
3. **Matching:** matching relationships such as capitals to states
4. **Fill-in-the-Blanks/Completion:** an incomplete statement
5. **Short Answer:** usually a direct question

Types of Authentic/Performance Assessment

1. **Essays:** choose topic of interest, research, write
2. **Performance Tasks:** writing a letter or magazine article, designing a travel brochure
3. **Exhibitions and Demonstrations:** science or math exhibition
4. **Portfolios:** art/poetry/writing/reflection works compiled
5. **Classroom Presentations and Oral Discourse:** mock parliament session or political campaign

There are many methods of evaluation. Too often when students and teachers hear the term evaluation, they immediately think of tests. However, there are many other ways to discover information about student progress and, in turn, to inform them of their progress. These other ways include checklists and anecdotal records, student-teacher conferences, portfolios, journals, and class presentations. It is important to evaluate student learning at a variety of levels. Not only is it important to assess how well students know and understand material presented, but you also need to find out how well they can apply concepts, analyze and evaluate concepts, and create new ideas. Generally, tests that use multiple choice, true and false, matching, and fill-in-the-blank types of questions can effectively assess student knowledge and comprehension. However, we need to question the validity of traditional paper and pencil tests to assess all learning.

Much student learning can be evaluated through other methods. We think that these methods are often more action-based, focusing on what students can and are doing or thinking. While these methods may not be directly "measurable" in the traditional sense, they can be authentic indicators of real learning. Below are a few areas where we believe students will benefit from a broader-based, more authentic assessment plan.

Constructing Knowledge: Students learn how to uncover knowledge and understanding for themselves.

Cooperative Learning: Students discover the benefits of working with others, compromising skills, etc.

Greater Accountability: Students assume more responsibility for their decisions.

Increased Self-Confidence: Because students will have a greater say in their learning, they become more self-confident and assured of their own abilities.

Tapping Creativity: Students begin to tap their own innate creative skills.

Self-Reflection: Students examine their own perceptions of many issues in society. As such, they begin to develop and reflect on their own judgments and thoughts.

Equal Opportunity: Students who do not perform well on selected response assessment practices because of different learning styles are given an opportunity to do what they can do instead of what they can't.

Learning Is Fun: Students have fun because they are not repeating the same tasks.

1. GENERAL OBSERVATION

Observation is an important part of the evaluation process. Observation helps us consider our students' mental, physical, or social activity while they are involved in an educational activity. By using observation as a component of the evaluation process, we are able to consider the whole child, rather than one aspect. Observation helps us consider the processes employed by the student, the attitudes displayed, and the effort given. By observing students as they work we can discover clues that help us encourage them individually.

Quoted below is a list of learning outcomes devised by Robert Linn and Norman Gronlund [see *Measurement and Assessment in Teaching.* (1995). 8th Ed. Upper Saddle River, NJ: Prentice-Hall, Inc.] that can be assessed by observation. While this checklist is not comprehensive, it does give an indication of student behaviors that you can observe and incorporate into your student evaluations.

Outcome	Representative Behaviors
Skills	Speaking, writing, listening, oral reading, performing laboratory experiments, drawing, playing a musical instrument, dancing, gymnastics, work skills, study skills, and social skills
Work Habits	Effectiveness in planning, use of time, use of equipment, use of resources, demonstration of such traits as initiative, creativity, persistence, dependability
Social Attitudes	Concern for the welfare of others, respect for laws, respect for the property of others, sensitivity to social issues, concern for social institutions, desire to work towards social improvement
Scientific Attitudes	Open-mindedness, willingness to suspend judgment, sensitivity to cause-effect relations, an inquiring mind
Academic Self-concept	Expressed as self-perceptions as a learner in particular subjects (e.g., math, reading) and, in general, willingness to attempt new problems
Interests	Expressed feelings towards various educational, mechanical, aesthetic, scientific, social, recreational, vocational activities
Appreciations	Feelings of satisfaction and enjoyment expressed towards nature, music, art, literature, physical skill, outstanding social contributions
Adjustments	Relationship to peers, reaction to praise and criticism, reaction to authority, emotional stability, social adaptability

The following is a checklist for general observations that a teacher might record in a class. The type of grid shown can help us keep current records of our observations. New descriptions can be added as the work within the classroom changes from student to student, as the year progresses, or as new objectives emerge. This chart can be adapted so that an individual student has room to document his or her growth over the year.

STUDENT OBSERVATION CHECKLIST					
Student Names/Dates					
Stays on task with a single book, article or assignment					
Chooses a variety of different materials to address the problem being studied					
Is able to choose the material to match the assigned task					
Responds in informal conferences about current work and the ways that materials are used					
Shows compassion for fictional characters, historical people, or classroom peers					
Demonstrates respect towards others					
Expresses an open and inquiring mind through comments and questions					
Shows an appreciation for nature and a concern for environmental matters					
Etc. — The possibilities are infinite and can be tailored to your own unique group of students.					

There are at least two advantages to using observation as a part of the evaluation process: (1) observation gives a wider range of information about the student that may not be evident through written work and (2) observation helps teachers to get to know students as individuals.

2. INTEREST SURVEY

Often the information gained from a student interest survey can help us to plan more effective lessons. Following is an interest survey that may be conducted. One disadvantage of using information obtained by observing students is that it is not directly "measurable" and can be difficult to translate as part of the grading process. This type of survey can help collect information about students' attitudes and interests. If used more than once during a year, it is possible to identify shifts in attitudes. Teachers should adapt the examples to reflect the interests of their own students.

Student Interest Survey

Directions: Check the box that best describes how you feel about the items listed:

Name_____ Date_____

	Like	Undecided	Don't Like
1. Solving puzzles			
2. Playing outdoor games			
3. Playing indoor games			
4. Writing letters and stories			
5. Reading romance stories			
6. Reading mystery stories			
7. Reading adventure stories			
8. Attending plays and theater			
9. Playing computer games			
10. Surfing the Internet			
11. Cooking			
12. Making Crafts			
13. Collecting things			
14. Reading magazines and newspaper			
15. Travel			
16. Playing music			
17. Reading about famous people			
18. Reading to young children			
19. Attending concerts			
20. Hanging out with friend			
21. Other			

3. ANECDOTAL RECORDS AND CHECKLISTS

Both can help teachers record their observations in a systematic way. Anecdotal records are a diary or log of student progress using written comments jotted down by the teacher. These records provide useful data for reporting to parents and to the students themselves. Checklists can record performance levels in a variety of situations and activities such as group participation, demonstration of understanding, and completion of tasks. Sample checklists are shown.

Anecdotal Record Form

An anecdotal record form can be an easy, efficient, and humanistic way to evaluate your students. We suggest that you have a number of blank forms close by so that you can jot down things that you have noted about particular students throughout the week. Below is an example of an anecdotal record form. Its purpose is two-fold. The teacher's notes can be incorporated into the student's assessment record, and the action plan is just that — a plan of action for both the teacher and the student.

Student: Imran Shiron
Date: 11/15/2000
Grade: 9
Place: student eating area

Incident

During lunch supervision, Imran asked me to read a poem that he had been working on. It was about war. Imran's poem reflects a sense of loss and isolation in youth today. The speaker contrasts the camaraderie of young soldiers during the second world war with that of young boys today who wander purposelessly through each day. I am astonished by Imran's use of complex vocabulary, and more importantly, by his sophistication in theme. I asked him if I could make a copy of the poem, but he declined, saying he did not feel it is good enough.

Action plan

Imran is a strong writer who does not yet believe or have confidence in his own ability. However, his willingness to show me the poem suggests that he is ready to begin writing more seriously. Needs a gentle nudge. Follow up with this in class. Talk to Imran about working independently on a writing assignment.

Observational Checklist Guide for Speaking

The Student:	Yes	No	Needs More Info
Is interested in sharing experiences orally			
Responds to ideas shared by others			
Exhibits confidence presenting ideas			
• to a partner			
• to the teacher			
• to a small group			
• to the class			
Speaks clearly			
Uses broad vocabulary			
Uses varied sentence patterns			
Speaks in complete sentences when appropriate			
Expands and elaborates ideas effectively			
Is able to organize ideas effectively			
Other aspects for observation 　1. 　2. 　3. 　4. 　5.			

Writing Checklist/Observation Guide
(for small groups or individual student assessment)

Evaluation strategies employed:
e. g. 1. Writing folders
      2. Journals
      3. Prompts for holistic scoring
      4. Group writing

	Often	**Sometimes**	**Seldom**
Is able to write effectively: • on self-selected topics • on assigned topics • when following a pattern or structure			

Strategies — is able to:
• use room resources to
    assist writing
• benefit from peer or
    teacher response
• revise a piece of writing
• use pre-writing strategies
    that have been modeled
• follow through a piece to
    completion			

In writing situations — is able to:
• write or print legibly
• use writing strategies that
    have been taught or modeled
• self-correct
• express ideas and feelings
    effectively
• use references and sources
    independently
• use invented spellings when
    it is appropriate
• use peer and class resources
    effectively			

Research Checklist

This type of checklist can provide teachers with an overview of a class and their students' ability to work through research techniques. Teachers can complement this checklist with other rater information.

STUDENTS' NAMES

Activity Being Done								
collecting								
interviewing								
ordering information								
planning								
recording								
reporting								
researching								
surveying								
organizing data								
writing up results								
presenting to others								
checking for errors								
using proper references								
etc.								

4. SELF-EVALUATION

Students and teachers can both be responsible for evaluation. Students are not alone in the need to assess their own performances. Teachers, too, can benefit from self-evaluation. Self-evaluation encourages students to be responsible for their learning and to be more reflective about what they learn. As teachers, we have to help students realize that they can learn from each other as well as the teacher. We can also help them become more knowledgeable by helping them take more responsibility for evaluating themselves as well as others. Giving students more responsibility is in itself an educational act. We can't just tell students to "Do it." Before students can take additional responsibilities, they need to more clearly understand the criteria for evaluating activities and assignments. The down-side of this need is that it takes time to teach students to have and to handle this responsibility. The up-side is that, when students understand the criteria for evaluation, they become more skilled and thoughtful scholars.

For example, students could use the following type of evaluation form to consider their own performance or the performance of their peers in a dramatic presentation, a debate, a poetry reading, or a multi-media performance.

Sample Checklist for Student Editors

1. Thought/Content		
Will the reader/listener find my work interesting?	___ yes	___ no
informative?	___ yes	___ no
funny?	___ yes	___ no
imaginative?	___ yes	___ no
Did I say what I wanted to say?	___ yes	___ no
When the reader/listener tells me about my piece, does what he/she says match what I was trying to do?	___ yes	___ no
Are any parts of the piece unclear, missing or confusing?	___ yes	___ no
Did I write too much about too many things and lose the focus of what I was saying?	___ yes	___ no
2. Organization		
Are my ideas in the correct order so that they make sense?	___ yes	___ no
Is there an effective beginning, middle, end?	___ yes	___ no
3. Effectiveness		
Can I combine some sentences?	___ yes	___ no
Can I expand some sentences or add important details?	___ yes	___ no
Have I used effective vocabulary?	___ yes	___ no
descriptive words	___ yes	___ no
action words	___ yes	___ no
connecting words	___ yes	___ no
Does my piece have a variety of sentences?	___ yes	___ no
long/short	___ yes	___ no
different beginnings	___ yes	___ no
complete sentences	___ yes	___ no
statements, questions, etc.	___ yes	___ no
4. Surface Features		
Does my piece have an appropriate title?	___ yes	___ no
Have I used capitals correctly?	___ yes	___ no
Have I checked punctuation carefully?	___ yes	___ no
Did I estimate the correct spelling?	___ yes	___ no
Have I underlined or circled words for checking?	___ yes	___ no

Students need to monitor their own speaking skills. The checklist that follows will helps students become better self-evaluators in this area. Teachers can adapt this checklist for their own needs.

Group Discussion Checklist for Self-Evaluation

Directions: Read each statement. Answer honestly. Put a checkmark in the space of those skills which you completed well.

1. _____ I came to the group discussion prepared with some ideas to share.

2. _____ I listened thoughtfully in my group.

3. _____ I can remember the other group members' ideas.

4. _____ I was open-minded when listening to the ideas of other people.

5. _____ I helped others by asking them questions about their ideas.

6. _____ I shared my ideas with others.

7. _____ I supported my ideas with specific points.

8. _____ I encouraged others in my group to give their ideas.

9. _____ Our group made a plan before it started to work.

10. _____ Our group attended to the task we set out.

11. _____ I learned something in my group.

12. _____ We fulfilled our task well.

13. Three ideas I took from the group were:
    (a)

    (b)

    (c)

14. Two ideas I contributed to the group were:
    (a)

    (b)

Students who are included systematically in their own evaluation not only improve their work, they also improve their critical abilities. Students can also help the teacher by working to evaluate their own work, the work of their peers, and the written products produced by professionals. The following overview contains general questions and criteria that would work in any subject area.

Evaluation Descriptors for Student Use

Content

    1. Does the report or written work make sense?   ___ yes   ___ no

    2. Are all the parts of the product clear?   ___ yes   ___ no

Development

    1. Is the report or written work complete?   ___ yes   ___ no

    2. Are the beginning and ending sensible?   ___ yes   ___ no

Sentence Structure

    1. Are the sentence length and type varied?   ___ yes   ___ no

Vocabulary

    1. Does the author use the "right" words?   ___ yes   ___ no

Conventions

    1. Is there enough space between words and lines of print so that the piece is easy to read?   ___ yes   ___ no

    2. Is the grammar correct?   ___ yes   ___ no

    3. Is punctuation used correctly?   ___ yes   ___ no

5. INTERVIEWS AND CONFERENCES

Talking with students can give us a great deal of valuable information that we might not get from their written work. Interviews and conferences can help us understand how students see things and, because they are interactive and dynamic, these conversations can help shape perspective and understandings through their natural give-and-take. Interviews and conferences can also help shape both student and teacher attitudes, highlight their questions and concerns, and help move the classroom experience in positive directions.

Teacher-student conferences can also offer information about student learning. Conferences can be brief and informal or formal and structured. Regardless of format, the information gained as a result of conversation can be invaluable in creating relationships and understanding between teachers and students.

Many questions or initiating comments may be helpful in beginning a conference with students. The questions asked should be authentic, should allow for

genuine responses to issues that are important to the student, should allow the teacher to contribute thoughts without constraining the student, and should focus on student work and ideas.

The following initiating comments and questions may be useful starters:

1. Tell me about what you're working on today.

2. I can see that you've tried ......, what gave you that idea?

3. How far have you come since our last conference? I seem to remember you working on....

4. Did you try that suggestion that Shaun gave in the small group conference the other day? How did it work?

5. What would you like me to focus on when I look at this piece of your work?

6. What have you been trying to include in this work?

7. As I listened to you it occurred to me that....

8. The aspect that seemed to come through so clearly in this piece of work was.... Was it something you have been working on?

9. What questions should I ask that I am forgetting?

10. What can you tell me that would better help me understand what is happening in the class?

11. What are you most proud of in this work?

12. What would you like to do better in this piece?

The following form can help students and teachers keep track of their interactions. As they confer over student work, they can note the main points of their conversations. The form helps check the progress of both student learning and the work that the student does on a particular project.

Record of Conferences

Skill/Learning Goal/Project/etc.	Date	Comments/Grades/ Progress Report
1) Content/Sense/Meaning		
2) Fluency		
3) Development/Organization		
4) Other Areas for Comments		

6. PORTFOLIO ASSESSMENT

This approach offers an alternative to the traditional "final exam" for evaluating student performance. Portfolios ensure that the teacher knows what the students are doing and learning, what the students understand about themselves as learners, and what the school values as formative information about student progress and about the programs being offered. As part of the portfolio assessment, students regularly contribute samples of their work and other anecdotal records of their experience to their portfolios. Teachers also contribute comments, suggestions, and formal evaluative reports. Both teachers and students are responsible for keeping the portfolios up-to-date, encouraging learning partnerships and sharing accountability. Students must learn to make responsible choices and to recognize that their improvements as learners and personal growth are real accomplishments. Portfolios can include any of the following materials:

1. cumulative reading logs
2. writing samples
3. long-term assignments and daily homework
4. tests
5. messages between teacher and student
6. activity logs
7. photos or drawings
8. peer evaluation reports
9. agendas/goals/work plans for independent studies
10. records of progress
11. communications with student parents
12. interim school reports
13. records of extracurricular activities
14. student self-evaluations
15. videotapes of learner presentations

Six Strategies to Maximize the Effectiveness of Portfolios

Fenwick and Parsons [see Fenwick, Tara and Parsons, Jim. (2000). *The Art of Evaluation: A Handbook for Educators and Trainers.* Toronto, ON: Thompson Educational Publishing, Inc.] suggest the following six strategies to help maximize the effectiveness of portfolios in evaluating students.

- Define the purpose of the portfolio.
- Teach the students to self-reflect.
- Structure portfolio reviews by the students.
- Make time for peer evaluation.
- Share portfolios with students regularly.
- Give yourself time to master portfolio use.

Sample Portfolio Assessment		
Name:	Date:	
1=Dependent 2=Limited 3=Adequate	4=Competent 5=Proficient 6=Superior	
Preparation of Portfolio Portfolio is complete — contains all required material Items are appropriately dated, identified, organized Portfolio contains Table of Contents Overall presentation shows care and thought Comments:	1 2 3 4 5 6	Weighting __
Documentation of Growth Work samples reflect growth in particular areas Portfolio items chosen thoughtfully and purposefully Portfolio demonstrates achievement in significant outcome areas of knowledge, skills, and attitudes Portfolio organization and presentation demonstrate awareness of identified audience needs Comments:	1 2 3 4 5 6	Weighting __
Evaluation of Selected Item(s) Overall quality Thoughtfulness: detail, clarity, originality, development Appropriateness of form for message and audience Relationship of form and content Use of details in presentation to enhance... (meaning, audience appeal, mood, design, unity, emphasis, voice, clarity, or whatever criteria are relevant to the item) Comments:	1 2 3 4 5 6	Weighting __
Quality of Reflections/Self-Evaluation (demonstrated at closing conference) Comments examine products as well as learning processes, strategies Comments show evidence of revisiting specific samples Comments show self-awareness and insight into behavior, attitudes, values, and beliefs Comments identify areas for further improvement and set directions for action and learning Comments:	1 2 3 4 5 6	Weighting __

*from *The Art of Evaluation: A Handbook for Educators and Trainers,* p. 150.

7. JOURNALS

Journals are another way for teachers to communicate with students and gain insights into their learning. A journal can take many forms, but the goal should be to provide students with a place to record their ideas, concerns, and opinions. Journals encourage written conversation between teachers and students, or between student and student, and should be assessed not for accuracy and perfection but for effort and thoughtfulness.

Journal Starters

These are some ideas identified by Fenwick and Parsons [Fenwick, Tara and Parsons, Jim. (2000). *The Art of Evaluation: A Handbook for Educators and Trainers*. Toronto, ON: Thompson Educational Publishing, Inc.] for your students to begin writing in their journals. While most of the starters are based on textual responses, you can adapt these to reflect your own purposes.

Personal responses might use starters such as:
- A central point to remember here is...
- An example from my own experience of one of the key points here is...
- Some questions raised for me are...
- A quotation that is important for me is... because...
- It is ironic that...
- Some things I didn't understand in this reading are...
- A new insight I had in this reading is...
- Some useful ideas from this material that I can apply to my own work are...
- Some implications of this article for issue I care about are...
- Some things I already knew that this article reinforces are...
- A pattern I notice is...

Critical responses to readings might use starters such as:
- A point I particularly disagree with in this article is... because...
- I agree that... because...
- The purposes seem to be...
- The context of this article is... which affects the message that...
- The author's point of view is...
- My reply to the author's point of view is... evident in...
- The target audience for this article seems to be...
- Some limitations of problems I see in this article are... This material is similar to or different from... because...

8. ASSESSMENT RUBRICS

Assessment rubrics are sets of guidelines that outline criteria for certain performance tasks. They are helpful for both students and teachers. When a rubric is given to students at the same time as the assignment (and we recommend this), students know beforehand what is expected of them and how their work will be

graded. For teachers, rubrics help keep their grading consistent and on track. Teachers can create descriptors that identify student performance as strong, proficient, or weak. These are generally referred to as holistic rubrics since they describe different levels of overall performance. Another type of rubric, known as an analytic scoring rubric, identifies and rates different criteria more specific to a performance task. Rubrics can be used for both formative and summative evaluation, providing students with information about their strengths as well as the areas that need attention. We have included a number of sample rubrics that you can adapt for your own classroom.

Chart for Noting Outcomes from Assessments

Assessment Outcomes	1 Weak	2 Basic	3 Proficient	4 Strong
	Little or no presence of the characteristic	Some (or beginning) visible presence of the characteristic	Detailed and consistent presence of the characteristic	Highly inventive and mature presence of the characteristic

A variety of evaluation forms are also available that can provide students with feedback and a more formal assessment. The two examples that follow are useful for evaluating oral presentations.

Oral Presentation Feedback Form and Evaluation Guideline

Topic/Assignment/Activity

Goal/Intent/Focus/Objective	1	2	3	4	Comments
Purpose 　Clearly stated 　Maintained 　Accomplished					
Organization 　Clear 　Effective					
Content 　Major Points Given 　Supporting Details 　Adequate elaboration					
Response to Listeners 　Eye contact 　Clarification 　　(if needed) 　Gestures and facial 　　expressions					
Voice Control 　For effective delivery					
Overall Impression					

Evaluating a Speech

Speaker_____ Title of Speech _____

General Impression	1	2	3	4
Content 1. Topic 2. Purpose 3. Details				
Organization 4. Introduction 5. Body 6. Conclusion				
Language 7. Vocabulary 8. Usage and style				
Voice 9. Control 10. Tone				
Diction 11. Articulation 12. Pronunciation 13. Phrasing and emphasizing 14. Tempo				
Physical Behavior 15. Poise 16. Gestures 17. Facial Expression				
Communication 18. Projection 19. Response				

9. ANALYTIC EVALUATION

Analytic evaluation is intended to direct the reader's attention to specific features of the writing and suggest point values for each feature. The grade is arrived at by summing scores on the subsections. This scoring tool is more specific than holistic marking because the rating guide defines and illustrates criteria for both writers and raters. These guides, when they are taught to students, help make the final grade more understandable. They also help students focus on their strengths and weaknesses as writers.

	Term1	Term 2	Term 3	Term 4
Content				
•main idea (theme)				
•coherence				
•cohesion				
•effective supporting ideas				
•response to assignment				
Organization				
•effective introduction				
•sequential development				
•closure/effective ending				
Matters of Choice				
•vivid/concise				
•varied				
•appropriate language or terms				
•vocabulary use				
•sentence structure				
•correctness				
•variety				
Corrections				
•capitalization				
•punctuation				
•spelling				
•paragraphs				
General Overall Impression				

Sample Performance Task with Analytic Scoring Rubric

Imagine you are a Canadian journalist on assignment in Japan. Your task is to write a newspaper article describing four agents of change in Japanese culture. Identify and define what each agent of change is, whether it is an internal or external agent of change, and what effect it has had on Japanese culture. In order to do your best, be sure to review the scoring rubric before you begin.

ANALYTIC SCORING RUBRIC

	Agents of Change	Specifics	Effects on Japanese Culture	Organization and Writing
4	Four major and important agents of change identified.	The specifics identified are relative to Japan and clearly support the major topic.	Article demonstrates a depth of understanding of the impact of change on Japanese culture.	The organization and writing is exemplary, detailed, and clear with few, if any, grammatical errors.
3	Most of the agents of change identified by the student are major and important ones.	Most of the specifics identified support the major topic.	Article demonstrates a reasonably good understanding of the impact of change on Japanese culture.	The organization and/or writing meets standards. There may be a few grammatical errors.
2	At least two of the agents of change identified are major.	The specifics identified may be mixed up or do not clearly support the topic.	Article shows a satisfactory understanding of the impact of change on Japanese culture.	The organization and/or writing is satisfactory. There may be more than a few grammatical errors.
1	At least one of the agents of change identified is major.	Few of the specifics identified support the topic.	Article does not show a clear understanding of the impact of change on Japanese culture.	The organization and/or writing may not meet standards. There may be many grammatical errors.

TESTS

TWO TERMS OFTEN USED when referring to tests are **criterion-referenced** and **norm-referenced**. Criterion-referenced tests are composed of items directly taught and determine student mastery of a unit of study. In other words, does the student know the items that the group has studied as part of the class content? Norm-referenced tests are standardized tests that relate student learning to that of other students of the same age and/or grade level. These tests are mostly made up of objective multiple choice questions answered on separate answer sheets. In other words, how does the learning of this one class compare to the learning of similar classes?

We have included the most familiar formats of test items, noting their limitations, strengths, and some general rules to follow when selecting these test formats. Alternative response, matching, and multiple-choice items require that students select an answer. Completion, short answer, and essay test items require students to supply the answer. All of these tests have their place, and as a teacher, it is important that you consider what your student-learning outcomes are and what test items will best measure these outcomes. In addition, consider your students' strengths and limitations. Some students prefer multiple-choice items while others are terror-ridden by the distracters in these questions. Some students excel in writing essays while others are panic-stricken by the mere thought of writing. For this reason, we suggest that you incorporate a variety of tests into your classroom, thus giving all students the opportunity to "strut their stuff" when their choice of testing presents itself and to improve upon the areas of testing they deem most fearful.

1. **True-false or alternative response items:** These generally consist of a declarative statement that the student is asked to mark true or false, correct or incorrect, yes or no, fact or opinion, agree or disagree. Although seemingly quick and easy to write, these are not always easy to prepare beyond the knowledge level (some exceptions to this are distinguishing between fact and opinion and identifying cause-and-effect relationships). These items allow a fifty percent chance of guessing correctly and do not provide teachers with any diagnostic information. Also, if a student marks an item as false, there is no evidence that the student knows what is correct. However, these items are useful when there are only two possible alternatives. In addition, a relatively large number of items can be answered in a typical testing period, and there is less of a demand on reading ability. Some suggestions for writing alternative response items follow:
   • the statements are clearly true or false, correct or incorrect, etc.
   • all statements are approximately the same length
   • there are approximately the same number of true as false statements
   • double-negative statements and other confusing questions are avoided
   • systematic patterns (TTFFTTFF) are avoided
   • terms denoting indefinite degree (large, regularly) are avoided
   • statements taken directly from a textbook are not taken out of context
   • the statements are kept short and use simple vocabulary and sentence structure
   • one central idea is included in each statement
   • specific determiners such as "usually" or "always" are avoided

2. **Matching items:** Like alternative-response items, matching questions are largely restricted to simple knowledge outcomes such as factual information based on simple associations (i.e., provinces and capital cities). It is often difficult to construct items that contain a sufficient number of homogeneous responses, often resulting in obvious clues. However, reading and response time is short, and scoring is easy, objective, and reliable. When developing matching items, use the following rules of thumb:
   • keep the descriptions and option lists short, homogeneous, and arranged in some logical order

- fit the items together on one page
- be sure the lists are titled
- make the distracters plausible
- include more options than descriptions
- put lists with the greatest amount of reading on the left and the responses column on the right
- state directions clearly (i.e., Can each response be used once or more than once?)
- ensure the items appropriately measure the intended learning outcomes

3. **Completion items:** Completion items can either be written as a question or an incomplete statement. Often it is difficult to phrase a statement so that only one answer is correct. In addition, completion items are not very adaptable to measuring complex learning outcomes. However, a broad range of knowledge outcomes can be measured, and guessing is not an issue. This type of question is well suited to computation problems and other learning outcomes where supplying the answer is important. Helpful hints for developing completion items are as follows:
   - be sure that the items require a single-word answer or a brief, definite statement
   - be sure the item poses a clear problem and provides structure for an answer
   - be sure that the students have had access to the answer
   - position the blank towards the end of the sentence

4. **Short-answer items:** Short answer items are similar to completion items in that students supply the answer. In a short answer, however, often more than a one-word answer is required. Scoring can be difficult in these items because answers can vary or be partially correct. While these items are generally unsuitable for measuring complex learning outcomes, they are good for measuring knowledge of terminology, specific facts, principles, methods or procedures, and simple interpretations of data. Suggestions for constructing short-answer items are as follows:
   - word the item so that the required answer is both brief and specific
   - a direct question is generally more desirable than an incomplete statement
   - indicate the type of answer you are looking for (i.e., numerical units, full title of poem and name of poet, etc.)

5. **Multiple-choice items:** Constructing good multiple-choice items can be time consuming because finding plausible distracters can be difficult. In addition, scores are often influenced by students' reading abilities. However, the strengths of multiple-choice items often outweigh the limitations. These items enable the measuring of higher-level cognitive objectives. A broad sample of student achievement can be measured, and incorrect alternatives can provide

teachers with diagnostic information. In addition, scoring is easy and objective and influenced less by guessing than true-false items. Some suggestions for writing multiple-choice items are as follows:

- design each item to measure an important learning outcome
- avoid clues in the statement portion (stem) such as the same word in both the stem and the option
- state the stem of the item in simple, clear language
- avoid grammatical clues (a/an, is/are)
- put as much of the wording as possible in the stem
- keep the length of the options similar
- use options such as "all of the above" sparingly
- be sure there is only one and clearly one best answer
- be sure all distracters are plausible
- use negative questions or statements only when the knowledge being tested requires it
- if you have to use negative wording, then clearly emphasize it (i.e., Which of the following did not occur during the Edo period?)
- include three to five options for each question

6. **Essay test items:** This is the most familiar form of performance-based assessment. What distinguishes the essay item from the test items already mentioned is the freedom of response. These items require that students compose an extensive response. Students must organize, integrate, and synthesize their knowledge, use information to solve new problems, and be original and innovative in problem solving. Poorly constructed essay items ask for recall information that is best answered by short answer, completion, or multiple choice. The limitations of essay test items are unreliability of scoring and the amount of time required for scoring. However, essay questions can measure complex learning outcomes not measurable by other test items, with an emphasis on integration and application of thinking and problem-solving skills. Essay items are easy to construct and have the added bonus of being able to evaluate writing skills. Suggestions for constructing essay questions are as follows:

- be specific about scoring criteria in advance of administering essay questions (If possible, include a scoring rubric directly on the test so that students know what is expected of them.)
- consider beforehand how to handle factors that are irrelevant to the learning outcomes being measured such as handwriting or inaccurate, off-topic, factual information that students throw into their answers
- restrict essay questions to those learning outcomes that cannot be measured satisfactorily by objective items
- construct questions that will call forth the skills specified in the learning outcomes

In a group of five or six, write your interpretation of the word "discuss." Share your meaning with the group. How many different interpretations of this one, commonly used word have arisen? How might each of your students interpret this word?

- phrase the question so that the student's task is clearly indicated (Be as specific as possible.)
- indicate an approximate time limit for each question so that students are able to budget their time
- when marking, evaluate all responses to one question before going on to the next one
- if especially important decisions are to be based on the results (i.e., if results are the deciding factor in whether the student goes into English 30 or 33), get a second marking opinion from another teacher
- if you are unable to think of one or two thesis statements for an essay based on the topic you have given your students, chances are that they too will have difficulty with this. In this case, rewrite the question or scratch it all together.

It is important to select *directing words* that are clear in their meaning. In order for words to be clear to students, they first have to be clear to us when we are creating questions. For example, consider the words in the following sentence. How exactly do you expect your students to answer questions that begin with these directions: explain, define, describe, compare, contrast, summarize, justify, interpret.

When developing your own tests, it's important to remember that tests should clearly link the material being instructed, in terms of content and format, with what is being evaluated. Tests should check for understanding and the ability to apply what has been taught. Your tests should reflect a variety of tasks and not rely too heavily on a question/answer format.

When putting your test together, consider the following suggestions:

- Group together items of similar format, so that only one set of directions is necessary for each format.
- Arrange test items from easy to hard, in order to build student confidence and reduce test anxiety.
- Space the items clearly.
- Keep items and the options on the same page, to prevent unnecessary flipping of pages.
- Check for randomness in the answer key, to avoid obvious patterns.
- Check test directions for clarity.
- Proofread the test carefully.

MANAGEMENT AND RECORD KEEPING

THE ORGANIZATIONAL ASPECTS of evaluation are crucial. Management procedures need to be as carefully considered as the instruction and evaluation procedures you choose for your classroom. Systematic data collection and recording help us to recognize patterns of behaviour, learning, and performance at both class and individual levels, and help teachers provide effective feedback to the students, the administration, and parents.

Record keeping procedures should accomplish several things. They should directly reflect both long and short term objectives of instruction. They should be manageable, efficient, and practical in terms of teacher and student time and energy. They should reflect a balanced consideration of a wide range of factors related to student progress, and the information should be as precise and systematic as possible. Our advice is to find and learn how to use a computer grading program to collect and store your grades. These programs are inexpensive, easy to use, quite easy to adapt, and can provide printouts of student grades. They can't do everything, but they are real time savers. We think no teacher should be without such a grading program.

To arrive at fair and objective grades, consider the following: (1) use a point system for grading, so that students always know where they stand; (2) determine point values for different assignments; (3) determine a policy for make-up work; (4) balance the final grade between homework, class work, quizzes, major tests, and assignments; (5) do not combine academic grades and behaviour/effort grades.

REFLECTING ON EVALUATION STRATEGIES

QUESTIONS TO CONSIDER **before** using an evaluation strategy:

1. Why am I using this particular type of evaluation?
2. Why am I evaluating the students at this time?
3. What do I expect to learn about the students as a result of this evaluation procedure?
4. What do I want the students to learn from this evaluation activity?
5. Does this evaluation method consider the objectives?
6. Have I adequately prepared my students for this type of evaluation procedure? Have I reviewed enough?
7. Have I accounted for the various ability levels and skills within this class?
8. Have I planned for time to do follow-up activities after the evaluation?
9. Have I taken the test to make sure that it is as free from problems as I can make it?
10. Is there something about the form of the test that makes it difficult for students?
11. Did I make the test easy to grade?

Questions to Consider Before You Attempt to Evaluate Student Progress:

14. How do you reward students for their efforts when their final product is not up to par?
15. Are students able to express what they think is important?

ACTIVITY:

Create five multiple choice questions based on the information in this chapter. Then create an essay-type question. Which is easier to create? Why? Which would be easier to evaluate or grade once the students had written the tests? Why?

ACTIVITY:

Role play a student/teacher conference. What will you ask the student? What role will you assume? Why?

ACTIVITY:

List criteria for good grading practices. Discuss in a group. List examples of inappropriate grading/evaluation practices. Discuss.

Questions to consider **after** using an evaluation strategy:

1. Did the students understand what was asked of them on the evaluation?
2. Do the results indicate that the students were prepared for this type of evaluation activity? How did the "good" students do?
3. If I use this evaluation procedure again, what changes will I make to it? Did I find mistakes that I need to fix for next time?
4. What other methods of evaluation might be more appropriate?
5. Were there questions that students missed that were my fault? If so, did I make up for it by giving them the benefit of the doubt?
6. Did the test differentiate between the students who prepared and those who did not?
7. Is there evidence of cheating? If so, what can I do about it?

THE TEACHER'S ROLE IN THE EVALUATION PROCESS

TEACHERS HAVE A VARIETY OF RESPONSIBILITIES in the evaluation process, including: 1) awareness of and response to current perspectives in curriculum and learning, 2) maintenance of a balanced viewpoint, and 3) connoisseurship. A connoisseur actively develops and refines the abilities needed to be observant, critical, and appreciative. Teachers must actively resist the temptation to view evaluation as focused solely on what students cannot do or understand. We need to be aware that we are concerned with the development and growth of each individual.

When teachers are connoisseurs and are supported by observational, measurement, diagnostic and descriptive information then their informed professional judgment must be acknowledged as valid within the overall evaluation program.

A FINAL WORD

RECENTLY, VIEWS OF EVALUATION and student assessment have changed. Educators have begun to realize the importance of including students in the evaluation and reporting process, rather than having these remain mysterious and unexplainable. Students are encouraged to attend parent/teacher conferences. Sometimes the students themselves conduct the conferences between the parent, teacher, and student. The student's work is the focal point of the conference, rather than the student her/himself. We admit that we have some mixed feelings about these new procedures. What do you think of this trend in evaluation and reporting processes? What are some of the up-sides, or potential benefits? What are some of the down-sides, or potential problems?

CHAPTER 3

APPROACHES TO LEARNING

INTRODUCTION

LEARNING CAN TAKE PLACE in a variety of situations. To learn implies that an individual gains new understanding or new knowledge. *Learning is an active process.* This statement may seem simple, but it contains two important elements: activity and process. Learning doesn't just happen without activity; and learning is organized in some way. This organization might be unconscious, but events don't just happen haphazardly. Events are attached to meaning.

Learning also implies another important element. *There is always a learner.* Again this sentence may sound extremely simplistic, but imagine what would happen if, as a teacher, you forgot that there were learners out there. Maybe you have already experienced a teacher who has taught as if there was no one learning.

To repeat: there is always a learner. The learning process and the content of learning are always influenced by the learner. Learning is a joint process between teacher and learner. Learning does not depend solely on what the teacher presents but is dependent upon both how the information is presented and how the learner processes that information.

LEARNING STYLES

WE'RE NOT SURE where the phrase learning styles came from, and it sounds a bit "fashionable" to us, but we will use it because everyone else in education seems to use it. Regardless of where the phrase came from, there are some important things to understand about learning styles. The first thing you should know about learning styles is that there are as many in your classroom as there

Situation Background: You are a first-year teacher teaching grade 10 math. Throughout junior high school, Sara has been a very good math student. But this year, in your class, her grades are slipping.

Case: Sara and Amanda are best friends, although they are very different in personality and work habits. Sara is not very talkative herself, but Amanda is. You hate seating plans, but for the sake of this one situation you'd even consider it. Every time Amanda turns around to talk to Sara, Sara is distracted. All year you have been wondering how to "get to her" without seeming like a nag. You want to just say, "Sara, Amanda is your friend and I don't want that to change, but get smart! Amanda is going to cost you a good grade."

When you were a student yourself, many of your friends were like Sara. They didn't cause the trouble; they just respond to their friends and get caught up in it. Sara is a good kid, she just doesn't seem to be able to figure out what's happening and what the cost will be to her grade-wise. How would you solve this "problem?"

are students. Each person is unique. All humans think and act differently. All have their own unique time, place, and style in which they work best. Why, then, write a chapter on learning styles? Because, within the multiplicity of learning styles there are also general aspects of learning that you need to think about when planning for and organizing classes.

When thinking about learning styles, it is important to consider the students themselves. Junior and senior high school students are immersed in various stages of adolescence. Most developmental psychologists call adolescence a difficult but exciting time in students' lives. Most teachers would agree.

Certain things tend to be true about adolescence. For example, during adolescence, peers gain greater importance than ever before, and adolescents would much rather spend time with their friends than with their parents. Adolescents need to come to terms with new things they are learning about their parents. For one thing, parents are less than perfect. Adolescents also need to determine their own individual set of moral, religious, ethical, and political principles. Adolescents are "coming to terms" with their own developing sexuality and the physiological changes brought on by puberty. They are also beginning to develop positive (we hope) personal relationships. Adolescents are beginning to think about the future, about career options and job possibilities, and are trying to forge a niche for themselves in the larger society. These characteristics endow the decisions that adolescents make with a sense of importance and mystery. Everything seems new, and there seems to be no rules to follow. At least adolescents need to learn these rules for themselves. This, often, includes rules about their own effective learning styles.

If you read about learning styles, you will see that they are usually defined as "cognitive, affective, and physiological traits of learners as they interact in the classroom environment." An individual learning style is defined as the preferred (or easiest) way that a person learns.

What is important to understand is that students with different learning styles understand educational problems in different ways and, as a result, try to solve the problems and content they face in school in different ways. It is also important to know that individual learning styles generally remain constant over time and are largely determined by both a student's mental capabilities and personality. While people do grow, mature, and change, discovering the way that a particular student learns best can help that person become a more successful learner throughout life.

A SCHOOL-BASED APPROACH TO LEARNING STYLES

BECAUSE MOST OF YOU will be concerned about how students with different learning styles can be taught, we will start by considering learning styles within the school. A **school-based approach** to divergent learning styles considers four distinct areas. Each of these areas affects how students respond to instruction.

1. **School environment:** What does each student think about school? What does each student believe is an ideal place to learn? For example, does the student like the room warm or cool, with lots of interaction with others or isolated and quiet? Some students do their homework best when loud music is blaring. Others are distracted by any noise at all.

2. **Emotional support:** How much emotional support does the student need? For example, some students are self-starters and self-directed learners. Some need their assignments divided into small pieces. Some need periodic due dates. Some turn in everything the next day. Some, for one reason or another, wilt if anyone looks directly at them. Some thrive on friendly, and sometimes not so friendly, confrontation. Emotionally, students differ. These emotional differences must be considered.

3. **Sociological composition:** The phrase sociological composition might seem a bit abstract, but what it really refers to is how students react to peer interaction. For example, does the student prefer to work alone? Does the student work best in a group? Will certain students ever be able to work together without causing an uproar? Can a student learn from another student, or does the student only trust learning from an adult? When considering a student's sociological composition, you must take into account how that student gets along with others in the class, with you as the teacher, and even with parents or other adults in his or her life.

4. **Personal or physical elements:** What is the student's most effective mode of learning? Is it visual or auditory? Does the student learn best by touching and working with concrete objects? Does the student have an active imagination and learn best by visualizing metaphorically? Does the student need to move around the classroom, or does the student need to sit still? And does the student learn best at a particular time of day, or week? There are, as you may well know, morning people and afternoon people. This physical aspect of learning can be very important.

LEARNING MODALITIES

LEARNING MODALITIES is another one of those phrases that sounds more complex than it actually is. Again, what you should understand is that learning modalities play an important role in students' chances of success in the classroom. People who work in the area of learning modalities suggest that humans use three basic modalities to process material into their memory: (1) visual (learning from seeing), (2) auditory (learning from hearing), and (3) kinesthetic (learning from touching, doing, moving). People generally have one predominant modality; however, many people have a balance between two or even all three senses. It is important that students are aware of their primary modality of learning so that they will know how to approach their own learning.

CHARACTERISTICS OF LEARNING MODALITIES

Visual	Auditory	Kinesthetic
• mind sometimes strays during verbal activities • finds verbal instructions difficult • doodles	• easily distracted by sounds	• taps pencil or foot while studying
• observes rather than talks or acts	• talks to self aloud • enjoys talking • enjoys listening activities	• likes to touch people when talking to them • enjoys physical rewards • enjoys handling objects • uses hands while talking • in motion most of the time
• organized in approach to tasks • uses advanced planning • meticulous, neat in appearance • notices details • has good handwriting		• dresses for comfort
• likes to read	• likes to be read to • enjoys music • hums or sings • whispers to self while reading	• reading is not a priority • enjoys doing activities • likes to solve problems by working through them
• usually a good speller	• may have some difficulty with spelling	• poor speller
• memorizes by seeing graphics and pictures • remembers faces	• memorizes by steps in a sequence	
• quiet by nature	• outgoing by nature	• outgoing by nature; • expresses emotions through physical means

SUGGESTED AIDS FOR LEARNING MODALITIES

BELOW, WE HAVE LISTED some suggestions for how you might modify your teaching as a response to different student learning modalities. Obviously, it is not always easy nor is it possible to adapt your teaching to each individual student in your classroom. The point is, however, that you should become more and more aware, as you work with your students, just how they learn best. We believe in a simple rule of thumb: every student should have the opportunity to learn in ways that he or she can master. In other words, just because it is easier to treat every student the same is no reason to do so; you need to give each student instruction in the different learning modality that best fits his or her easiest way to learn. Visual learners should have their day in the sun, as should auditory learners, as should kinesthetic learners. If you do not, you are "cheating" students. In short, if you ignore their preferred styles and they don't learn, it's not their fault — it's yours.

MODIFYING TEACHING IN RESPONSE TO LEARNING MODALITIES

Visual	Auditory	Kinesthetic
• use guided imagery • use photographs • demonstrate • use exhibits • form pictures in your mind • draw or use drawings • take notes • use cue words • see parts of words	• use tapes • read aloud • talk to yourself • use oral directions • repeat things orally • sound words	• physically do it • practice by repeated motion • pace or walk while studying • stretch, move in chair • write • take notes • associate feelings with concept information • write on surfaces with fingers
• use colour codes	• use rhythmic sounds • make up poems of rhymes	• exercise, dance
• use notebooks • use study cards • use charts, graphs, maps	• have discussions	• write lists repeatedly
• watch TV • watch filmstrips, movies	• watch TV • listen to music	• role play
• use mnemonics (acronyms, visual chains, mind maps, acrostics, hook-ups)	• use mnemonics (word links, rhymes, poems, lyrics)	• use mnemonics (word links, rhymes, poems, lyrics)

There are many little quizzes that can help suggest individual preferences or attractions to different learning styles. Although most of these are done by so-called experts, you don't have to be an expert to think the concepts through. Probably you can do almost as good a job as the experts. And, at the same time, you can learn more about these ways of learning.

Here's your task. In a group of 3-4 people, review the learning styles' charts just presented in this chapter. Create a Likert-type scale (agree-neutral-disagree) self-test for other students with 25 statements that you believe would help reveal individual preferences for learning styles. When you have finished, make enough copies of your self-test to share with another group in your class. You take their self-test; they will take yours. Answer the statements honestly. When you have finished, review your own test and talk with others about their tests. What have you learned about your own learning styles and the learning styles of others?

GREGORC'S LEARNING STYLES

ONE OF THE MOST INFLUENTIAL EDUCATORS in the area of learning styles is Anthony Gregorc. Gregorc's **style delineator approach** is based on his research studies of the functions of the left and right hemispheres of the brain. His system focuses on the implications of these different brain functions for perceiving and ordering. Perceiving simply means to see. A student can either see in ways that are concrete-oriented (prefers input through the physical senses) or are abstract-oriented (prefers logical, deductive modes of learning). Ordering simply means to make sense of what one sees. Ordering can be either sequential (a systematic, step-by-step presentation) or random (an unorganized, simultaneous display of information).

Gregorc's four categories may seem theoretical and difficult at first; however, they are really quite easy to figure out and quite useful when you realize that they are based on some simple ideas about the ways that learners perceive and order. The four categories of learning styles, developed from Gregorc's preferences, are listed and explained in the table that follows.

Gregorc's Four Learning Styles	How the Student Learns
Concrete Sequential	The student learns in linear, sequential ways. The best learning is concrete learning.
Abstract Sequential	The student learns in abstract, analytical ways. The student prefers a mentally stimulating, but ordered, learning environment.
Abstract Random	The student learns in emotional, imaginative ways. The student prefers an active, colorful, and free learning environment.
Concrete Random	The student learns in concrete ways. The student prefers a world of activity that is nonlinear and intuitive. The student also prefers a stimulus-rich, problem-solving learning environment.

REAY'S CLASSIFICATION OF LEARNERS

DAVID REAY [see Reay, D.G. (1994.) *Understanding How People Learn*. New Jersey: Nichols Publishing Company] suggests that there are four identifiable types of learners. He classifies learners as activists, reflectors, theorists, or pragmatists. Although most individuals will prefer one style of learning, Reay says that learning is most effective when learners (students) develop skills in all four styles, described in the following quoted table.

Type of Learner	Characteristics	Wants	Instructional Approaches
Activists	impetuous, impatient, unafraid of error, open-minded, flexible	experience, variety, excitement, activity, people	group-based, experiential, learning by doing, group reviews, lively debate
Reflectors	cautious, careful, methodical, good listener, judicious	objective data to draw conclusions, chance to reflect, analyze and deliberate	distance learning, private study, audio, video
Theorists	rational, logical, disciplined, inquisitive, objective	models, theorems, complexity, perfection, rationality, coherence	computer-based training, electronic interactivity, models, simulators
Pragmatists	planner, practical and down to earth, experimental	chance to experiment, new ideas, theories and techniques, practical applications, solutions to problems	controlled experience, personal coaching, on-the-job training

ACCOMMODATING LEARNING STYLES

WHEN THINKING ABOUT LEARNING STYLES, we believe that there are two important points to remember: (1) people learn in a variety of ways, and (2) each person has stronger and weaker modalities (visual, auditory, or kinesthetic). As we have mentioned before, students learn better in some ways than they do in others. You probably know your own learning preferences. And because you were obviously successful in school (or else you wouldn't be reading this book), the school and the classrooms where you learned somehow met your learning needs. You were a successful student. But, remember, not all students are similar to you. Some, in fact most, need more help than you did.

It is one thing to think like a student; it is another thing to think like a teacher. You are studying to be a teacher. And because you are, you must consider learning styles from the viewpoint of a teacher. As a classroom teacher, there are at least two questions that you must ask yourself. First, should you adapt your instruction to accommodate individual learning styles? Second, are you able to adapt your instruction to accommodate individual learning styles?

The answers to these questions might seem apparent. You are probably already saying, "Of course, we should consider how students learn best and adapt, if we can, our classrooms to these styles." And you are probably correct. At least, that would seem to be the obvious answer. But let's take a look at it from another perspective and ask a difficult question: are we "short-changing" our students if we always allow or encourage them to work from their positions of strength? Would it be better to encourage, maybe sometimes even force, them to strengthen and

develop areas that are their weaknesses rather than continuing to develop their strengths? Is part of learning becoming well-rounded? Perhaps we should be broadening the learning experiences and abilities of students by "forcing" them to adapt to alternative styles. We will help you grapple with this statement later in the chapter.

ORGANIZING COGNITIVE THINKING

IF YOU ARE GOING TO BE SUCCESSFUL teaching students, you must become more aware of the hierarchical levels of cognitive thought and you must use these levels as a way to organize your teaching. Did that sentence sound like something straight from a textbook — more confusing than enlightening? Again, the sentence is more difficult sounding than it is difficult to understand. We play these little word games sometimes with you because we hope, as you read books and journal articles in your chosen area of teaching, that you don't get lost in the verbiage. If nothing else, we want you to remember that most ideas about teaching are more simple than they are complex. What makes educational ideas difficult is they are hard to implement, because you are dealing with dynamic learners.

Hierarchical levels of cognitive thought simply means that the way students think, or could think, can be organized into levels — from simple to complex. Some learning tasks are easier and more simple than others. Some learning tasks can only happen when other, lower level learning tasks have taken place. Some ways of learning build on building blocks of a simpler way of learning. In short, whenever a hierarchy of learning has been developed, someone has thought about learning from a particular perspective and has organized learning tasks into levels — usually from simple to complex.

The most well-known and one of the most useful systems of organizing cognitive thinking is Bloom's Taxonomy. This classification scheme is concerned with the acquisition and manipulation of factual information. According to Bloom, there are three domains of learning — the cognitive, the affective, and the psychomotor. The cognitive domain can be divided into six major levels. The chart that follows outlines the six levels and provides you with a number of verbs that will help you assist learners to explore a variety of cognitive learnings at each of these levels.

These six levels are often simplified into three more general categories — Knowledge/Comprehension, Application, and Problem Solving. These cognitive domain activities can also be compared to the affective and the psychomotor domains. This comparison can be helpful when you consider how you might teach in the areas of values, attitudes, or physical activities. The charts that follow will give you a sense of how taxonomies can be helpful when stating objectives in all three domains — cognitive, affective, and psychomotor.

BLOOM'S TAXONOMY OF THE COGNITIVE DOMAIN
1. knowledge: gain specific facts, ideas, vocabulary, etc. *Key Verbs* — list, match, write, recall, know, who, what, where, when, recite, memorize, name, group, find, identify, label, choose, pick, fill in, underline
2. comprehension: grasp meaning of material learned; communicate learnings and interpret learnings *Key Verbs* — group, define, show, summarize, re-word, retell, extend, reorganize, change, expand, demonstrate, translate, outline, explain, account for
3. application: making use of learned knowledge in new or concrete manner, or to solve problems *Key Verbs* — apply, select, model, classify, record, demonstrate through, put to use, interview, experiment, solve by, put together, utilize, choose, organize
4. analysis: taking ideas, learnings apart, separating into component parts, seeing relationships; finding unique characteristics *Key Verbs* — divide, break down, uncover, survey, simplify, contrast, classify, search, compare, analyze, inspect, take apart, discover, categorize, sort, examine
5. synthesis: reorganizing parts to create new, original things, ideas, concepts; stress of creative behaviors *Key Verbs* — create, form, develop, build, invent, make up, compose, design, originate, imagine, construct, devise, produce, blend, re-arrange, predict, suppose
6. evaluation: making judgments or decisions based on chosen criteria, standards, conditions *Key Verbs* — rank, judge, rate, determine, conclude, evaluate, measure, justify, award, defend, decide, criticize, assess, grade, recommend

Sometimes all this talk about stating objectives can become a foreign language to students. Just what do you do when you state objectives? I'm a teacher, not an "objective stater," you may wonder. Here's where the previous charts can be very practical and helpful to you as a teacher.

SAMPLE VERBS FOR STATING LEARNING OBJECTIVES

Knowledge/Comprehension Levels

Cognitive Domain	Affective Domain	Psychomotor Domain
arrange, classify, define, describe, distinguish, defend, explain, express, identify, list, locate, match, name, order, outline, quote, recall, recite, record, relate, reproduce, report, response, review, state, select, summarize, underline	arrange, classify, define, describe, distinguish, defend, explain, express, identify, list, locate, match, name, order, outline, quote, recall, recite, record, relate, reproduce, report, response, review, state, select, summarize, underline	begin, choose, complete, demonstrate, hear, identify, manipulate, move, point to, press, push, select, set up, show, sort, specify, touch

Application Levels

Cognitive Domain	Affective Domain	Psychomotor Domain
apply, assemble, calculate, choose, compute, define, demonstrate, discover, draft, draw, estimate, explain, extend, illustrate, infer, interpret, manipulate, modify, operate, practice, predict, prepare, produce, relate, schedule, show, solve, use	adhere, affirm, approve, assist, commend, complete, comply, describe, discuss, form, invite, join, justify, perform, practice, propose, select, share, study, work	activate, adjust, assemble, build, calibrate, construct, copy, demonstrate, dismantle, display, disconnect, draw, execute, load, locate, loosen, manipulate, measure, open, operate, perform, remove, replace, rotate, select, slide

Problem-Solving Levels

Cognitive Domain	Affective Domain	Psychomotor Domain
analyze, appraise, arrange, assemble, break down, categorize, choose, combine, compare, compose, construct, contrast, convert, create, criticize, defend, devise, diagram, differentiate, estimate, explain, formulate, generate, illustrate, infer, interpret, justify, manage, modify, organize, plan, predict, prepare, rate, relate, solve, support, tell, value	act, adapt, change, defend, display, influence, integrate, organize, revise, solve, use, verif	arrange, adapt, combine, compose, construct, create, design, diagram, illustrate, modify, organize, plan, repair, service

When you are thinking about the activities or lessons you will teach your students, how do you know what to do. Sure, on a theoretical level you agree with all the ideas we have stated in this chapter and you want your teaching to be both valuable to the class and adapted to the individual needs of the students in your class. Here's where we would suggest you start. Every activity you create to teach is just that — an activity. It is active. You will notice that the chart is full of verbs. Look at the chart, notice that all these words are action words. Some may not make immediate sense to you. In other words, you may not know yet how to turn that action word into a classroom activity. If we were you, we would keep this little chart around when we were teaching. When we were thinking about tomorrow's or the next day's lesson plan, we would review this chart looking for verbs (action words) around which we could build the lesson plan. We would try to make choices from all three domains. If we could do this, we would be pretty sure that we were developing lesson plans that would at least begin to attend to the variety of needs of students in the class we were teaching.

BEAUCHAMP AND PARSONS' LEVELS OF UNDERSTANDING

THERE ARE A NUMBER OF DIFFERENT TAXONOMIES, or hierarchies of learning. Beauchamp and Parsons [Beauchamp, L. & Parsons, J. (1995). *Teaching from the Inside Out*. Edmonton, AB: Duval House Publishing] have outlined a different taxonomy for helping organize thinking about materials being studied. Unlike Bloom's Taxonomy, which focuses on learning without suggesting what students might do with what they learn, Beauchamp and Parsons believe that learning starts with understanding what might be done but realizing that everything that is done also has a political agenda. In other words, Bloom's taxonomy does not distinguish between action that is "good" or "bad," "worthwhile" or "worthless."

Beauchamp and Parsons, however, take a stand about "goodness" and "badness," or about "worthiness" or "worthlessness." Their taxonomy is based on the belief that the end (or highest level) of learning is worthwhile action. They believe that there is always a moral center to teaching, that education is not just "busy work." Unlike Bloom's Taxonomy, the levels of understanding in Beauchamp and Parsons' taxonomy include encouraging students to make decisions about what they learn and to take action based on their decisions. They build their system around four basic activities: (1) focusing; (2) layering; (3) extending; and, (4) deciding. Like Bloom's Taxonomy, Beauchamp and Parsons' taxonomy is hierarchical. That is, focusing is a first-level (or basic) activity; deciding is a fourth-level (or more complex) activity. One is not better than the other; and all the levels are needed. However, it would be difficult to make decisions without having gathered information in other ways. Good decisions are based, in part, on good understanding.

Group Activity

Get together with three other people in your class. Working together, use the verbs on the charts above to outline a number of lesson plans that you could teach. Try working in a variety of different subject areas — you never know what you might be asked to teach. Work on some of the easier verbs; then pick some of the verbs that are more difficult. When you are finished, have at least 12 quick lesson outlines completed. Using a jigsaw or another cooperative activities framework, be ready to share these with others in your class. Take notes on the best outlines you hear. (A word of vigilance. Remember, you are preparing to become a good teacher. You should create some way of saving the very best ideas you hear or have. These will help you immensely when you come to teach your own classroom.)

What Do You Think?

When we talk with education students, there is a general agreement that learning should have a political agenda. That is, generally speaking, what a person learns should be used to make the world a better place in which to live. Although Beauchamp and Parsons' taxonomy may be appealing, it is important to think through the implications of what they say. For a teacher, what are the good points about such a stance? What are the bad points? For example, many people shy away from such a political stand because it is difficult to know who should make decisions about what is good action and what is bad action. Think through the problems. Write notes for two sides of the argument. Then take a stand for yourself: should learning have a political agenda or should it stay away from questions of "good," "bad," or "worth?"

Beauchamp and Parsons' levels of understanding can be used to shape the way students answer questions. They uses four headings: **focusing, layering, extending, deciding**. Samples of these types of questions follow.

(Note: the following questions are examples of how to use questions with particular pieces of literature. In this case, questions are used to study the book *Dragonwings*, by Lawrence Yep, about a young Chinese boy and his father who build an airplane in 19th century San Francisco. But, these same sorts of questions could be used with any focus or in any subject area.)

Focusing: a focusing question focuses on the book or story. Its purpose is to help students find out more about the focus. As students answer the question, they study what is happening as part of the content.

Example #1: Focusing: individual student writing
When he first went to live in San Francisco, Moon Shadow met and lived with "The Company." Here he found some distinctly different individuals. Briefly describe three members of The Company, making sure to show how they were different from each other.

Example #2: Focusing: individual student and group activity
Many readers would see this story as a clash between the Chinese culture and the white culture. But this story is one where many different cultures clash against each other. Besides the Chinese-white cultures, there are also the cultures of strangers-hosts, good people-bad people, fear-courage, the superior person-the regular person, dragons-the crowd, and those with dreams-those without dreams. Choose three of these clashing cultures. Create a chart highlighting some of the important characteristics of each culture you choose. Discuss your charts with other people in your group. Do you agree with each other's suggestions?

Layering: a layering question goes past the book or story into life. Its purpose is to help students think of other circumstances that are similar to those in the story. It asks the student to consider how what is happening in the story is similar to real life.

Example #1: Layering: individual student activity
Things have changed in the United States and Canada since this story took place. How have thoughts and feelings about Chinese (and other racial minorities) changed? Have laws changed? What do you think

caused those changes? Do the changes mean there is no longer any racial discrimination?

Example #2: Layering and extending: individual student writing
Imagine that a new person, straight from China, joined your class this morning. Describe what happened during the first fifteen minutes. Write down what you thought and how you felt. What does this tell you about your attitudes?

Extending: extending questions extend past the book or story right into a student's life. They are more personal than layering questions, and they ask students to understand how what is happening in the book affects what is happening in their lives, and vice versa.

Example #1: Extending: individual student writing
Prejudice is "pre-judging" a group of people (or individuals belonging to that group) on the basis of what you think are the characteristics of the group. Think about some people you are prejudiced against. What has caused your prejudice? Write down how and why you treat them differently.

Example #2: Extending: individual student writing
Have you ever felt that someone was prejudiced against you? What happened to make you feel this way? Try to put yourself back into the experience and describe what you thought and felt. Share what you write with someone else if you wish.

Deciding: deciding questions ask students to consider how what is happening in the book or story encourages or helps them make decisions about life and how they should live. The purpose of a deciding question is to help students make decisions, evaluate decisions, and make commitments to act on things that they have learned.

Example #1: Deciding: individual student activity
Do you often see members of other groups as all the same? What could you do to see each person as a distinct individual?

Example #2: Layering and deciding: group activity
In your group, organize a debate on the topic: "The qualities of superior people are most important in our society or the qualities of common people are most important in our society."

The purpose of these questions is to dig into subject area content with a purpose of accepting what you learn as information toward making changes in your life in the society in which you live. Unlike Bloom's Taxonomy, Beauchamp and Parsons' taxonomy has an implicit ideal of social and political action. The end of education, so say Beauchamp and Parsons, is not simply to know but to make the world a better place in which to live.

A FINAL WORD

AS WE MENTIONED before, making decisions about how to use the knowledge we have about learning styles can be more difficult than it seems at first glance. Earlier, we suggested that creating lesson plans where students might work at their strengths can be limiting. Now, let us sit on the other side of the fence.

We know that a body of research supports a high correlation between learning and self-esteem. In other words, the more a student regards himself or herself as strong, capable, and intelligent the greater that student's potential for learning. Simply stated, students who believe they are capable will learn more than students who believe they are not capable.

Here's the dilemma. Although it is important to help students become flexible and adaptive, are we doing so at the expense of their self-esteem? Is the focus on flexibility (on encouraging students to grow stronger, even by struggling, in their area of weakness) causing students to feel unsuccessful and frustrated?

More and more teachers are recognizing the individuality of their students and trying to accommodate personal needs. A large body of research has provided new understandings about how the brain works in general and how each brain works specifically. Teachers are developing a wide repertoire of teaching strategies and using them to produce more student success in learning situations. It's worth thinking about. How are you going to approach the fact that different students have different abilities and different ways of learning? Are you going to make learning political or are you going to ignore social action and concentrate on helping your students learn as much as possible, challenging them later to make decisions for their own lives and the society in which they live? These are some of the questions you must ask yourselves sooner or later in your work as a teacher. We encourage you to ask and answer them sooner.

CHAPTER 4

CLASSROOM MANAGEMENT

INTRODUCTION

THE SUCCESS AND SURVIVAL of a teacher often depend on classroom management skills. Yet, classroom management is one of the most difficult tasks any teacher faces. One reason "managing" a classroom is tough is because it is difficult to pinpoint exactly what classroom management skills involve or look like. It is also difficult to know why some things work and others don't. And the fact is that certain things work for some people and in some situations also complicates classroom life. But even if it were possible to know what classroom management skills looked like, the job would not be half over. It is even harder to "learn" classroom management skills. Some teachers struggle with classroom management for their entire teaching careers — and these can be good teachers!

COMPLEXITIES OF CLASSROOM MANAGEMENT

IT IS RELATIVELY SIMPLE TO OBSERVE a classroom and to analyze what is going on there. It may also be relatively simple to discuss effective approaches to each one of the activities you watch. But it is more difficult to understand why certain activities take place and why certain things "work." To complicate things further, those involved in the activities that take place often aren't really able to explain what is going on and why things happen in particular ways. Some very good teachers would be hard-pressed to explain their success as teachers and as

Something to Think About

Enter into any elementary or junior high school and stick your head in a classroom door. What do you see? You see, usually, one teacher and more than thirty students. So what?

Think about it. There is great significance in what happens each day in a typical classroom — thirty young people and one adult. And, surprisingly, the students are usually being directed and managed by this teacher — often a person not many years older than the students in the class. Sometimes it seems like parents and the rest of the public (in public education) forget just how difficult this aspect of teaching is. Sometimes it seems that parents and the rest of the public fail to appreciate the skill and determination involved in the activity of classroom management. One wonders why, especially when one often sees these same parents struggling with just one cranky and tired five-year old in the local grocery store. How selective is the memory of the public?

classroom managers. And even it they could explain their success to you, it is not clear that the things that work for them could be adapted to work for you.

As a beginning teacher, it is helpful to watch and think about how life in a classroom works. When you are considering the actions of a classroom, we believe the first truth to remember is that none of the activities you are viewing are played out in isolation. Formal (school-based and school-generated) and informal (for example, student group orientations such as preps, jocks, nerds, skaters, headbangers, etc.) organizational strategies are interwoven with discipline strategies. These weavings then collide with behavioral expectations from teachers, students, and classroom rules. These expectations and rules then affect and are affected by the physical layout of the classroom.

The whole process, when you consider it, sounds pretty complex. But, for experienced teachers, the process happens quite naturally — almost without notice. Of course, beginning teachers aren't so lucky.

So, here you are, faced with the difficult task of learning about classroom management. How can you, or any other beginning teacher, learn about classroom management? Listening to an "expert" lecturing about classroom management techniques is often less than helpful. How can someone who doesn't seem to have any problems help someone who has many problems? Furthermore, no two sets of problems are alike — or, are they? It's hard to know.

Although it's important to consider different approaches and strategies for "managing" students and classrooms, it's difficult to absorb expertise in management strategies through someone else's experiences. Still, having said that, we are going to try to address some of the issues involved in classroom management just that way — through our understanding of our own experiences. We might not be able to help you solve all your problems, in fact we are sure that we cannot; but we believe that what we have to say will help you prepare yourself as student teachers for your field experiences.

If you are one of those teachers, and there are some, who seem to have few management problems, don't get too confident. And never think that, having completed a course in classroom management, you will be able to smoothly tackle any situation that arises in the classroom. There is not a single teacher in any North American school who never has management problems — not a single teacher. It simply doesn't happen. First, all teachers are human and all humans make mistakes. Second, kids are kids. That thought might strike fear into the hearts of teachers; but, honestly, for us, we wouldn't want kids to be any different. Their dynamic nature makes them difficult, but it also makes them exciting to be around. One reason we like kids so much is that they are kids.

To coordinate all the activities that go on in a classroom takes experience, insight, and sensitivity. These traits can only be gained by acting and working in classrooms with students, by making mistakes and experiencing success, by vowing that you will never make this mistake again and by foolishly forgetting what got you into trouble and doing it anyway, and by finally learning the hard way from each mistake you make and each success you have.

Observing Space Arrangements in Different Classrooms

Directions: Observe the use of space in a variety of classrooms in a school. Draw diagrams of the classrooms, and observe students' movements in the spaces available to them. Compare the different arrangements you observe. Consider the following: What are the dominant methods of instruction in the classroom? How much movement is there among the students in the class? When do they tend to move around the most? Are there areas of the classroom that are used more, or less, than other areas? Could more of the spaces be effectively utilized? What does the arrangement of the classroom tell you about the way the teacher likes to work?

Face it. Accept it. Live with it. You will make mistakes, and you will suffer for them. Learn from your mistakes. But hope that when you make mistakes you don't harm anyone — including yourself. Here's the promise; if you have a well-managed classroom, you will likely have success in teaching.

BEING IN CHARGE

ONE OF THE MOST IMPORTANT ASPECTS of classroom management for beginning teachers is the feeling of being in charge and of having some semblance of control. You need to know that when unexpected situations arise you will be able to deal with them confidently. You need to learn to think on your feet; you need to have a variety of strategies to draw from; and you need to be flexible enough to implement what you know.

This "feeling of being in charge" comes when you have proven to yourself that you can deal with situations that spring up before you. But you have to do some background work in order to be prepared to deal with diverse situations. You should have considered the following things:

1. situations that are likely (or even possible) to come up during the course of a class;
2. the strategies that might possibly work in the event of these situations occurring;
3. the options open to you that will be condoned and supported by the school or system administration;
4. the nature of the student(s) you are dealing with;
5. the nature of the community with which you are dealing; and
6. the strategies that you would be most comfortable in implementing.

CLASSROOM SPACE

TRY TO IMAGINE WHAT AN EFFECTIVE CLASSROOM would look like. Begin with the physical characteristics of the classroom. Try to picture the walls, the arrangement of desks in the class, the displays that enhance the room's appearance, the bookshelves, the blackboards, the reading corner. Imagine what the students are doing in the class. Imagine what you are doing as the teacher. Where would you position yourself? What are the students working on? Consider the reasons for the room's appearance — how does the physical classroom enhance your effectiveness as a teacher?

The physical environment of your classroom is important for learning. For example, the heating of the room can affect your students' behavior. A hot or cold classroom often leads to cranky and distracted students. In this case, we suggest you open windows (if there are any) or remind students to bring sweaters. The noise level of a classroom is also worth noting. Some teachers prefer to keep their classroom doors shut during class time in order to minimize noises coming from the hallway, especially during test times. Often students themselves will shut the door if the outside noise level is bothering them.

While heating and ventilation systems and noise factors are often out of your control, the physical setup of your classroom is something you can work with. Some teachers prefer to have pictures, posters, and bulletin boards on display on the walls of their classrooms. This is generally the norm in elementary schools; however, the walls of secondary school classrooms are commonly bare. We think that a classroom, regardless of the age of the students, needs to be decorated. Often the best way to do this is to invite the students to become involved in the decor of the room by displaying their artwork or creating bright bulletin boards, theme walls, or even movie posters. The possibilities are endless.

Likewise, there are many different ways of organizing students' seating. Most teachers have a preference about the seating arrangements of their students. Some like straight rows, while others prefer desks arranged in groups of four or large semicircles. Some teachers like to assign seats and prefer that students remain in their seats during instruction. Other teachers invite students to arrange their own seating and maybe even encourage students to move physically throughout the room during instruction. Most often, seating arrangements coincide with individual teaching styles. For example, a teacher who moves throughout the room may prefer a semi-circle arrangement in order to have an effective "runway" for movement. Other teachers prefer rows because they feel they are less distracting for students. As you begin to identify and shape your own style, you will discover your preference for seating arrangements. The key, we think, is creating an environment that is warm and inviting — a place that is conducive to learning.

EFFECTIVE TEACHERS

THERE IS A SIMPLE, BUT IMPORTANT, QUESTION you need to answer: What qualities and skills does an effective teacher possess? Take a minute to remember your most effective teachers and list the qualities that made them stand out. After making this list, jot down the qualities you have found in effective teachers. Share these with someone in your class. How close are your lists? Can you get a pretty good picture of what "effective" means?

Although effective teachers have many different characteristics, when students we know talk about good teachers they mention some things over and over. Effective teachers listen to and hear what their students say, think, and feel. Effective teachers attend to their students' feelings as well as their thoughts; they understand their students' hopes as well as society's hopes for them. Effective teachers do not allow teaching to become routine. They know what their students need, and they know what it will take to gain the cooperation of the students. Effective teachers see and respect individuality; they respect all students. Effective teachers continually rethink and revise their teaching. Effective teachers avoid confrontation and power struggles. They try to respond to students as professionals.

Effective teachers are sensitive not only to verbal cues, but also to non-verbal messages being sent by students. "Body language" can give important messages to teachers who are able to "read" it. Not only can they understand their students better by reading their non-verbal language, but they can use it to more effectively manage their classes. Proximity and eye contact are two subtle but effective ways of sending messages to students who may be acting or speaking inappropriately. Tone of voice and gesture are slightly more obvious ways of communicating with students.

Students, too, send messages non-verbally. They can show their appreciation or their distaste of classroom activities with facial expressions and body posture. They can send messages by making or avoiding eye contact. Their tone of voice, too, can convey their thoughts and feelings.

Other attributes of effective teachers are that they:

1. establish and maintain rules and procedures,
2. present clear, smooth lessons that contain variety and challenge but are appropriate to the abilities of their students,
3. make themselves available to their students for extra help,
4. monitor students and hold them accountable for their work,
5. do not switch back and forth between instruction and behavior management,
6. do not punish the whole class for the disruptive behavior of one student,
7. match the pace of instruction to the needs of the students,
8. respond to unforeseen events and the needs of individual students,
9. involve the students as much as possible and allow time to think when asking questions,
10. know the names and strengths of each of their students.

These attributes are only some of the characteristics of an effective teacher. There are many others. Teachers, like students, are individuals; they bring unique strengths and interests to their classrooms. It is important to remember that no teacher has all of the qualities mentioned above. It is also important, however, to use characteristics such as these as a checklist to which you should aspire. The important question for you, right now is: What are your particular unique qualities and strengths? It is important to identify these strengths if you are to develop a well-managed classroom that suits your personality and strengths.

Non-verbal Communication

The following activities can be used to practice non-verbal communication.
1. Carry on a conversation with someone who is wearing sunglasses. Talk about how it felt not to be able to see your partner's eyes.
2. Try to continue a conversation with your hands in your pockets or behind your back. Does the lack of hands change the conversation in any way?
3. Repeat a variety of sentences with different tones of voice. For example, try saying, "What is wrong with you?", "This is wonderful", "You're terrible!", and "This is the best I've ever seen." using different voice qualities.

Who Are You?

Write a character sketch about yourself. (a) Forget about teaching for a moment. What are your best qualities as a person (pleasant personality, stick-to-it-ness)? What are your worst qualities (lack of organization, shyness, a tendency to be lazy)? List five of each (good and bad) qualities. (b) Now think about teaching. Transfer the notes you wrote into a teaching situation. For each good quality, write one practical way that quality will help you as a teacher. For each bad quality, write one way you can overcome it. (For example, if you stutter, you can work hard to develop small workable group strategies to get you out of stressful situations.)

Remembering Your Own Experience

In a small group, list the rules that your teachers used. Individually, for each person in the group, try to come up with four different rules. (a) From this list, list the five rules that are most common. (b) Also list the five rules you think are best for grade 3; for grade 6; for grade 9; for grade 12. Briefly, outline a rationale for changing these rules.

YOUR CLASSROOM RULES

NO MATTER HOW MUCH YOU TRY to anticipate problems that might happen in your classroom, situations will always arise during the course of a lesson for which you are not ready. Some of these situations are mildly annoying and harmless; some are untenable and must be stopped immediately. The simplest way to stop problems is to tell your students what you expect before problems occur. A well thought-out and simple set of rules helps students understand your expectations. These rules also help students take responsibility if they choose to ignore your rules.

Your rules should be based on your beliefs about teaching and also on the particular teaching situation in which you find yourself. It is important that you think about both your beliefs and the situation in which you teach before creating rules. For example, don't establish rules that you don't believe in just because someone else has those rules. This doesn't mean that you shouldn't think about establishing an experienced teacher's rule against, for example, students leaving the classroom whenever they want — even if you think students should have greater freedom. You should consider carefully the implications of living with, or without, certain rules. For another example, if you cannot enforce a rule, for one reason or another, it is better not to make it — even if you think the rule is a good one.

We would like to make some general comments about rules. First, you should develop rules that lead to student success, not to student failure. Second, you should state rules in positive not negative terms. "Show respect for all members of the class" is a more positive rule than "No put-downs."

Of course, the creation of rules must consider the stage of development of your students. For example, a grade two class is made up of grade two students. You should remember that grade two students would find the rule "Show respect" to be just a little abstract. In this particular case, "Do not call other students names." is a much more concrete and acceptable rule for grade 2. But grade 10 students would have an easier time understanding the abstract notion of "respect." We would encourage you to get student input into the formation of classroom rules. Students need to feel a sense of ownership for the creation of rules and a sense of responsibility for following them.

Once a reasonable and workable set of rules has been established, you need to consider how students will be held accountable for adhering to the rules, or what should happen if a student breaks a rule. How will you monitor student behavior? The consequences of breaking a rule should always be reasonable and "fit the crime." When students have direct input into the development of consequences, often they will support and cooperate by trying to follow the rules that everyone has agreed upon. This eliminates the habit of "crabbing" and "nagging" into which some teachers fall.

You must always ask questions about any consequences you outline for breaking rules. For example, will the consequences cause more problems than solutions? What are the likely disruptions that you will experience as a teacher? Will you be able to enforce your rules? Will parents or administration support your rules? And will you be the one suffering the most by the consequences? (For example, if you enforce a rule by having students stay after school, guess who is going to stay with them.)

DISRUPTIONS IN THE CLASSROOM

LIFE IN THE CLASSROOM is sometimes like a three-ring circus. Disruptions pop out of the shadows. Just when you think something else could never happen, guess what? It does. You need to be prepared for the little ups and downs of classroom life. But, just how prepared are you for the variety of disruptions that you will experience as a teacher? One way to prepare is to consider what could happen before it does happen. The following are examples of situations that might arise in a class that would cause disruptions:

1. students arriving late
2. students talking out of turn during a discussion, individual activity, or lecture (either to other students, or to you as teacher)
3. students coming unprepared (their homework is not done, their supplies are not with them)
4. students who are not willing to become involved in activities
5. challenges to your position of authority and responsibility
6. "playing" with materials such as pens, white-out, erasers, notebook covers, glue or scissors
7. students rocking on their chairs, falling out of desks
8. inappropriate dress or language
9. students who are under the influence of drugs/alcohol
10. students who are clearly emotionally distraught

We guarantee that, at one time or another, you will have students behaving in all of the ways listed above. Consider each of the behaviors separately and add any other problems you have seen in your experiences as a student. Then, ask yourself: What would I do if a student arrived at my classroom door late? ten seconds late? five minutes late? polite? surly? when you had already begun an activity? for the first time? again? as always?

In answering these questions, ask yourself: What do I need to consider? Here are some suggestions: how do the disruptions affect the rest of the class? What are the reasons for the lateness? What is the attitude of the student arriving late? How regular is this behavior? What rules have already been established regarding this infraction? How much flexibility do I have in making a decision? What are my options? Are there different options for different circumstances? Is treating students the same always fair? Can I follow through with the consequences established? Do I need to apply the same consequences each time?

The ten situations listed are typical problems a teacher might face. In a small group, make a general rule that would cover each problem. Then, in one paragraph, describe an incident that might occur. Trade your incidents. Solve the immediate problem put forth in that incident. Work on a plan of action that attempts to eliminate these problems in your classroom. Answer the question: what can be done to eliminate problems before they occur?

Consider the following scenario. How would you handle the situation?

Joe Lucci is older than most of the other boys in grade 7. He also can't read. But, it seems, for the first time he is experiencing some success. In fact, his grandmother called you out of the blue just to say that Joe is feeling so good about school that she can't believe it. You see, the grandmother adds, Joe hasn't felt good since his mother took off to Winnipeg to "find a job, and send for him later." That was six years ago, and Joe hasn't heard from his mother yet.

Joe surprised you last week when he announced, positively for a change, that he was going to finally pass on his report card this time. He had figured it out, and it looked like a piece of cake. Joe was beaming. You checked it out yourself, just to make sure; and, Joe was right. For the first time, he had a chance to pass. All he needed was to pass the final unit test.

After the test, you couldn't wait to grade Joe's exam. Joe had studied hard, you knew, and he was anxious to hear. In fact, unlike you, you promised to call Joe as soon as you had graded his test. When you finished Joe's exam, you were horrified. He had failed — just barely — but he had failed. What can you do? Passing would have meant so much to Joe. It might turn his life around. All he needed was five extra marks. Should you "cheat?" Or should Joe get what "he deserves?" What does the word "deserves" mean in this situation? in other situations?

ESTABLISHING ROUTINES

ESTABLISHING BASIC STRUCTURES AND ROUTINES helps students achieve success. It also helps maintain a positive atmosphere in the classroom. Routines and structures are like chalk lines around a baseball field. They help students know where the boundaries are. Without rules, students are left on their own to anticipate your requests. And because they are young and immature — characteristics that represent the age of students and which should not be considered sins — students will often be lost and uncomfortable. Structure is a necessary thing for students. It helps them attend to learning.

How do you gain the attention of your students? How do you begin or end a classroom activity? How do you manage classroom discussions? Although a variety of activities is essential, a basic classroom structure enables students to feel secure and know what to expect. Will you greet students at the door? Will you begin class by taking attendance? Will you pose a question of the day? Will you read a passage to them? When you ask them to read silently, do you mean it? Do you expect them to sit in assigned seats? When you ask for homework, what will you do if they "forget?"

Days that vary from a standard routine will often feel more chaotic, both for the students and for the teacher. If you move to a different classroom or if you rearrange the furniture or student seating plan, students will react. A fire drill, a school assembly, or an upcoming holiday is an event that encourages student reactions. If you can account for these variances in student behavior, you will save yourself a great deal of stress. Expecting students to work intensely on a difficult assignment if they are dressed in Halloween garb is not a good idea. Beginning a new activity five minutes before the end of the class might not be considered a good idea. You will soon learn that it is a better idea to plan active lessons for dress-up days or to play a review game for the last five minutes of the class.

You are the most important role model for your students. If you establish rules for your classroom, you are bound to them yourself. You also model appropriate and desirable behaviors such as respect, politeness, listening, and effective work habits.

If you expect students to hand assignments in on time, you should grade and return them on time. If you expect students to write effective stories, essays, poems, you should show them your own writing. If you use abbreviations on the board, they will use abbreviations on their paper. If your handouts are sloppy, they will turn in sloppy papers. Consider what you expect from your students. Are these expectations reasonable? Can you live up to them as well? Whatever you ask them to do, you had better be willing to do.

You should also attempt to help your students develop self-control. Self-control involves both visible (behavioral) components and invisible ones (emotions, understanding, and attitude). Students must believe that their effort results in success or failure; their success must be in their control. It should not be based on things that they cannot control, like ability, luck, or task difficulty.

PROACTIVE DISCIPLINE

OF ALL THE ASPECTS of classroom management, discipline is the prime concern for most beginning teachers. "What will I do if the students don't behave?" is the question almost all beginning teachers ask. When answering this question, it is necessary to consider two different angles of discipline (1) positive and proactive discipline practices and (2) holding students accountable for misbehavior.

Positive and proactive discipline practices are, of course, the most desirable ways to handle discipline problems. By positive and proactive discipline practices, we mean solving problems before they happen. The reason you should work to solve problems before they occur is quite simple and should almost go without saying. If you solve a problem before it happens, you don't have a problem.

But using positive and proactive discipline practices is not always possible. Despite your rigorous thinking and your considered discipline plan, students will always break your rules, challenge your authority, disrupt your class, and embarrass you in front of the principal and other teachers. And they will do it when you least need the hassles.

Still, you must try to forget that you are essentially working with dynamic young people (in other words, potentially explosive young time bombs) and try to solve problems before they happen. Of course, you will not always be successful; but, you will sometimes be successful. The more success you have in this area, the easier it will be for you to teach.

We know one thing: it is possible for you to think clearly through your discipline plan, classroom rules, and expectations. It is possible to develop rules that help students achieve success. And, in general, it is possible to encourage cooperation and trust in your classroom. You can and should encourage students to work with you to implement the kinds of rules that will build a positive classroom.

To build this positive classroom, you should consider the following questions:

1. What do I expect from my students? Are these reasonable expectations?
2. How will I communicate my expectations to students in a way that does not make me look like a dictator and that allows for student voice in my classroom?
3. What will be the consequences of not attending to my class expectations and rules? Are these consequences reasonable and are they possible to carry out?
4. When will I elicit the help of the administration in solving my discipline problems? What kind of support should I expect, and will I ask for?

The second type of discipline concerns, holding students accountable for misbehavior, are not as easy to prepare for. These situations usually arise at the most inopportune times, and you must make quick and astute decisions. You don't want to look foolish or make the student look foolish. Remember: in the middle of the action, it is difficult to remain calm and think rationally. It is especially dif-

Strategies for teaching self-control include: 1) self-monitoring, 2) self-talk (positive messages to oneself), and 3) teaching specific strategies for solving personal and social problems. Working together in a small group, list five activities that can be used to teach the three areas listed here. Make sure you outline one activity for each area.

Even though you cannot prepare for these situations before they occur, you can think about what you might do. And you can consider the following advice:

1. avoid situations of power challenge if at all possible,
2. ignore minor infractions of classroom rules,
3. begin with low-key responses (eye contact, proximity, mentioning the student's name),
4. do not put a student in a position where his or her only option is to display negative behavior. Remove the student from the spotlight position first,
5. use humor whenever possible to diffuse tense situations,
6. use punishment only as a last resort,
7. administer discipline procedures in a neutral and fair manner, focusing on the offensive behavior rather than on the student.

Study the list above. Are there any pieces of advice you might add? Discuss this list with teachers you know and have had as a student. Are there any pieces of advice these teachers would add?

ficult when you are being challenged or put in a difficult position. Better to expect that sometimes you will be stretched and be ready to react calmly than to not be prepared and then overreact or react too quickly, before you think.

When mentally preparing to deal with discipline matters, you may wish to consider the following questions:

1. Why is this behavior offensive to me? Does the behavior have anything to do with the personality of the student? Does the behavior have anything to do with my mood? Does the behavior have anything to do with the student's mood?
2. Am I overreacting? If not, how can I deal with this situation without either the student or myself looking bad?
3. What consequences are set out in my classroom rules? How will I apply and enforce these consequences?

Remember that, although it may be difficult now to imagine yourself being confident enough to handle the discipline matters that experienced teachers face, the more you face discipline problems and deal with them effectively, the more your confidence builds. It is better to hope for trials and successes rather than to hope for no trials. Without teaching experience, it is difficult to learn.

PUNISHING BEHAVIOR

CONSIDER THE FOLLOWING two simple guidelines for rewarding and punishing behaviors. If you do not reinforce a behavior, it will probably stop. If you reinforce a behavior, it will probably continue. Here are some suggestions for rewarding behavior:

1. Reward both the quality of the performance, and the participation.
2. Present rewards as natural or logical consequences of the desired behavior, not as manipulation of behavior. Students usually see tangible rewards that are not logically related to the behavior as manipulative.
3. Reward immediately.
4. Use specific rewards.
5. Use rewards that are meaningful and varied. Effectiveness is diminished if the rewards are predictable or expected.

Here are some guidelines for considering how to punish behavior:

1. Logically relate the punishment to the misbehavior.
2. The severity of the punishment should fit the seriousness of the offense.
3. The punishment should help the student understand the misbehavior and its consequences and make a commitment to change the behavior.

4. When punishing, clearly note what the desired behavior should be.
5. State clearly in advance what the punishment will be. Avoid empty threats.
6. Whenever possible, follow through on the punishment immediately. Always consider the dignity of the student.
7. Use demerit or check systems for repeated violations; however, only use these systems for readily observable behaviors. Consistency is crucial.

APPROACHES TO DISCIPLINE

THERE ARE MANY APPROACHES TO DISCIPLINE. Choosing one approach instead of another depends on your philosophical understandings, the nature of the students with whom you are dealing, and the situation in which you are involved. Some of the approaches you will read about if you do a review of discipline or classroom management include:

1. **Behavior modification:** Behavior modification is a system of positive reinforcement or reward. Its theoretical basis rests in the work of B.F. Skinner.

2. **Assertive discipline:** Assertive discipline centers on orderly classrooms, consistent teachers able to communicate clear expectations, behavioral limits and consequences, and the willingness to follow through on what is stated.

3. **Logical consequences:** Logical consequences is a democratic discipline approach where student participation is solicited in setting behavioral standards, expectations, rules and consequences. The logical consequences approach attempts to raise student consciousness about expectations, helps make students become more capable of recognizing their own motivations, and encourages them to "self-correct" misbehaviors such as (1) attention getting, (2) power seeking, (3) revenge, and (4) displaying one's inadequacies.

4. **Control theory:** Control theory rests on the belief that behavioral problems arise when the four inherent fundamental needs of students (to belong, to have power, to be free, to have fun) are not met. The goal in control theory is to introduce a self-management that enhances the quality of life for the total student community.

Obviously, there is more to these theories than we have presented here. Each of them has been expanded into full-blown and somewhat complex protocols for behavior. It would take years to read all there is to know about discipline or classroom management. You simply don't have the time. Plus, we don't think you need to know all there is to know. We think you need to work out a system of doing things that fit your beliefs, your situation, and your experience.

The Physical Arrangement of a Classroom

The physical arrangement of the classroom helps you create a classroom that operates smoothly. Is the room free of congestion? Are all students visible? Are materials available to the students? Can students see the action? The physical arrangement of the furniture reinforces the climate and atmosphere of your classroom and can help you create a comfortable and supportive space for the students and for yourself.

Struck By Her Own Words

Miss Cappella was having a tough time keeping her grade 8 students attentive to the lesson she was teaching. Partly, it was her own fault because she hadn't planned well enough. The weekend had sneaked by and she had had too little time to prepare the lesson she had wanted to do.

Finally, in frustration with Bill's antics, she stopped the whole class and announced to Bill. "Listen, I've had about enough. I'm going to call your parents after school and tell them what's going on."

"Go ahead, call them." Bill answered and went and wrote a phone number on the board.

"No, I mean it." Miss Cappella yelled. "I'll drive to your house and talk with them about you."

"Go ahead," Bill answered again and went to the blackboard and drew a map.

Miss Cappella knew in her mind that she was stuck. She had no intention of either calling or going to Bill's parents; she was just trying to shut him up. "What should I do?" Miss Cappella asked herself as Bill was walking back to his seat.

What should Miss Cappella do?

MANAGING A CLASSROOM

BECOMING A GOOD CLASSROOM MANAGER is a practical task. All the theories in the world will not organize and structure your classroom. You have to do it yourself. Because discipline is a practical matter and not a philosophical one, the philosophy of discipline you adopt will probably be pragmatic. It will combine a variety of these theories as well as many other discipline ideas you will pick up along the way. What is important to understand about discipline is that unresolved discipline issues will drain your energy and your spirit.

You've got to solve your own problems.

We mentioned earlier that teachers make hundreds of decisions every day. Once you begin to teach, you will believe it. Most decisions are minor, but every once in a while you will be forced to make a snap decision that has major consequences. Scary, isn't it? But you can prepare — a little. If you have already thought about your options and about your beliefs, you will be more prepared to make effective decisions that you can live with. It won't be perfect (it never is), but it will be a positive start.

"Withitness" is a term that has been coined to refer to your ability to have an overview of what is really happening in your class. This overview, if you can gain it, helps you notice problems and undesirable activities that should not escape your attention. Withitness helps you develop a positive classroom with an interpersonal climate that is amiable and respectful. Withitness helps you develop your students' worth and dignity, the approximation of democracy, and the understanding that forgiving mistakes and providing fresh starts must always be available.

Consider your own sense of withitness as you evaluate your teaching performances. Are your students interested and motivated? Is the topic relevant to them? Which students are struggling to keep up? Which students are bored? Is there any behavior you want to curtail? Are you asking each of your students to respond to discussions, or selecting the same few? Are you asking both males and females? Are you aware of restraints that some students may feel because of culture differences, ability differences, gender differences? Does your seating arrangement allow for all students to feel as if they are part of the group? Where do you stand when you teach? Do you move around or stay in one place? Do you have habits that students might find annoying or funny?

"Overlapping" is the ability of the teacher to manage more than one situation at one time. Once you see how many things happen in your classroom, you will understand that overlapping is a quality that is often necessary. For example, you will be greeted at your classroom door by several students all asking for your assistance, just as your principal calls you over the intercom telling you that you need to get in your absence sheet, just as Kim asks when she can make up a test, just as you wonder where you put your glasses, just as you notice that Pierre is looking at his marks in your grade book. You have ten actions, at least, to perform in the next few seconds if you are to control your class. And you need to learn how to deal with them all in a short space of time.

MOTIVATION AND MANAGEMENT

THERE IS A CLOSE RELATIONSHIP between your behavior as a teacher and your students' learning successes. You must structure activities that afford success for all students into your lesson plans. Here are some suggestions for encouraging success: (1) praise sincerely and often, (2) show respect for your students, (3) hold high expectations for all of your students, (4) be your real self, (5) avoid using sarcasm and negative comments.

There is also a relationship between a student's motivation and the teacher's knowledge of the student. If you know about a student's interests and strengths outside the classroom, this information can help you enhance and support that student's learning in your subject area; it helps boost the student's ego, and it helps begin a cycle of success for the student and for the teacher.

It is important to let students know at the beginning of the year that they cannot be passive participants in your classroom. Their interests, needs, and aspirations will be part of the material you present during the year. Then, you must allow students to make some choices or contributions in instructional materials, topics to be covered, and learning methods. You can motivate learners for active engagement in learning by using (1) contracts, (2) games and simulations, (3) self-paced, programmed texts, (4) grouping, (5) student volunteers, and (6) grades and tests. Be warned, however, that tests and grades are only motivation when their difficulty level allows for moderate to high rates of success. When students do poorly repeatedly on exams or get poor grades, even when they work hard, they soon become dis-motivated. When the going gets tough, most students will quit. We honestly can't blame students for giving up in situations where they can't win, no matter what they do — and, unfortunately, many classrooms are like this.

Not all motivations are as formal as the ones previously suggested. More informal types of motivation include: (1) praise and encouragement of student achievement that is immediately and honestly given, (2) explanations that give perspective to assignments enabling students to feel respected and valued, and that reduce the rigid teacher-student authority structure, (3) offering help that reduces the anxiety and self-doubt of students in their ability to start and complete tasks, (4) acceptance of diversity that shows students your unconditional acceptance of their diverse lifestyles, attitudes, and values, and (5) emphasis on rewards rather than punishments.

This informal motivation can help you establish a warm and supportive classroom climate. When students want to be successful, it is easier to motivate them. As their teacher, you need to consider how to best help develop and foster your students' desire to succeed.

The better that you know your students, the easier it will be for you to understand their needs and desires. One way to see different sides of your students is to participate in or observe them in extra-curricular activities. By watching them play basketball, or listening to them play the French horn, or by watching their dramatic performances you have a chance to learn valuable information about your students. Students will also appreciate your effort and interest, and your

Making Your Own Lists

Throughout this chapter, we have given you our best advice about classroom management. This advice is based on our more than eighty years of collective experience of teaching young people. But there's one problem with our experience. You're not us, and what works for us may not work for you.

Create your own list of rules — ones that you believe will work for you. You may use some of ours, if you want; but, your rules should not be our rules.

Ordering Your Actions

In this paragraph, several actions were listed. How, in order of importance, would you respond to what has happened in your classroom?

Consider a typical forty-minute period in a classroom. List some of the decisions that you might be called upon to make during one class period.

Did you consider what to do with a student who asks to go to her locker to get her pen? The student who asks to borrow a book? The request to alter an assignment, delay the due date, hand in a hand-written copy?

What about the student who just wrote all over her desk? Passed a note? Asks for help with yesterday's assignment? What will you do with a student who arrives late without an excuse? Or the one who just hurled an insult at a classmate?

Each decision you make, of course, alters all your subsequent decisions. Your ability to remain flexible, adaptable, and calm is crucial to your successful completion of the lesson. You may find yourself on a different instructional or discipline path than you had originally anticipated, and you will have to continue assessing the class and making decisions. It will help if you can continue to keep your goals and intents clear in your mind. Continually ask yourself, "Is this activity or direction going to get us to our ultimate destination?" This type of orderly and organized thinking will keep you focused.

new insights into their interests and personalities will give you valuable information for helping them succeed in your classroom. You will be able to begin on a positive note, discussing their interests with them, praising them for successes, and learning more about their strengths.

PLANNING FOR MANAGEMENT

ALTHOUGH THIS CHAPTER is not specifically about lesson planning, there are many links between effective planning and effective management. Plan a supportive learning environment before you begin your teaching assignment. Arrange the physical environment. Develop long and short-term plans that will achieve learning outcomes, engage student attention, and increase class cohesiveness. One simple way to do these things is to vary the lesson format and the student response patterns that you expect.

Before you begin teaching, develop an accountability system for managing student work. Be sure to review school policies to ensure your procedures are congruent with your school's policies. Consider a general grading system, the number, timing, type, and weight of long-term assignments; the frequency, nature, and importance of homework; the method of communicating assignments (including communicating to previously absent students); your feedback procedures; the monitoring of student achievement and how this will be shared with parents; and the system for dealing with late, incomplete, or missing papers. As you become more comfortable in your teaching, your classes will begin to flow, and your pacing will become more comfortable and natural. You will use transitions to move the students from one activity to another smoothly.

Pacing is important for classroom management. Students work best when they are actively engaged in their learning, without feeling bored or rushed. Good pacing helps you sense when students have had enough time to complete an assignment, or when they are frustrated and need more time.

Pacing helps you "fly by the seat of your pants," adjusting your classes accordingly to what you see. If you attend thoughtfully to what is happening, you will soon come to know if students find a task interesting; and, if not, you will know to move on. You will know that some students can handle greater challenges than others, that some levels of frustration are higher than others, that some students need more time than others. You will know how much repetition to build into your teaching, and how much is too much. You will have a variety of assignments to offer students, and you will know how much cooperation and how much competition encourages the most effective learning. You will know that everyone in the class, including yourself, will feel more satisfied if there is some sense of closure, whether it is a repetition of directions, a review of the lesson, or some other form of wrap-up.

As you become involved in classroom situations, during your field experience or at other times, you should observe what experienced teachers do to develop a positive learning environment. One of the best ways to observe is to focus only on certain teacher or student behaviors. You can even focus on one particular student. You may choose to observe only certain "skills" such as questioning techniques and evaluation methods. It will be impossible to observe everything that goes on in a classroom. Focusing on particular aspects of the teacher's performance will help you observe and record your own observations.

One aspect of teaching that has been mentioned previously but cannot have enough press is the use of humor. Teachers need to laugh at themselves, to be able to see when a situation is funny, ironic, silly, and just not terribly important. Sometimes teachers get themselves into all sorts of trouble by making too much of some insignificant event.

If you are going to be a good teacher, you will need to remember that even though the subject you are teaching is important, there are many other important things in the lives of your students. Life should be placed in perspective. "Don't sweat the little things" is probably good advice. When something happens, breathe deeply three times before your respond. Often what seems to be a giant at first turns out to be a shadow on closer inspection. Humor can diffuse a tense situation, relax students, and regain lost ground. Use it often.

INTERACTING POSITIVELY WITH STUDENTS

WE BELIEVE THAT THE FOLLOWING SUGGESTIONS will help you establish more positive and personal connections with students.

1. Make personal contacts with students you meet in hallways and classrooms; start conversations with individuals.
2. Use journals — write regularly to each student; no corrections, students simply answer your questions and ask questions.
3. Attend activities of student interest — watch intramural games, go to an event away from the school; go outside for recess or lunch breaks. Get to know students outside class.
4. Display student work — create bulletin boards and displays outside the classroom; share student work with the principal, other teachers and classes, and visitors. Celebrate the student successes.
5. Find out the interests of students — give out a questionnaire, listen to student conversations, have discussions with parents. Then incorporate what you find out into your classroom.
6. Adapt your curriculum to meet the interests and abilities of the students, individualize the curriculum to match student needs.
7. Create an inviting atmosphere — show dignity and respect for students by modeling, decorating the room, creating a quiet zone, creating a place to store individual materials, teaching and enforcing rules for keeping your

Cumulative Records: Should You Peek?

To look or not to look; that is the question. One issue that many teachers face is whether to look at the cumulative records of their students at the beginning of the year. On one hand, looking at the records of students is helpful. Sometimes these records give information that is very helpful in the task of teaching a particular student. For example, a student might have a serious disability or medical problem that a teacher should understand and attend to. On the other hand, knowing too much will shape your reactions to students. For example, if the records say that the student is a discipline problem, you will probably approach the student with a suspicious eye.

What do you think? Should you look at the cumulative records or should you leave them alone? In class, prepare and conduct a debate on the topic. Resolved: Teachers should look at the files of each student before teaching that student. In preparing for the debate, list arguments for both sides.

classroom a positive place, creating centers for writing, discussing problems, listening, viewing, and having students create displays.

8. Develop and reward the class for improvements — this gives students a common goal to work toward and increases the chances of developing group cohesion.

9. Read to students — have students pick a topic or book of interest, integrate the book into themes and use reading as a reward for positive work habits.

10. Teach social skills — create opportunities for success by teaching students how to avoid misbehaviors and how to interact in a positive manner.

11. Show interest and pride in students — introduce students to visitors, have students introduce class to visitors, ask students questions about their accomplishments, have slogans for the class, create lessons around student interests.

12. Share classroom time with students — create a time to discuss things of interest to students where they set the agenda, develop rules to maintain a safe environment, and encourage opinion and comments from other students.

CLASS MANAGEMENT TIPS (WHAT WORKS FOR REAL TEACHERS)

THE FOLLOWING TIPS come from real teachers. Each one represents the management ideas of a teacher, in his or her own words. As you read, try to make sense for yourself of what the teacher is saying . Can you turn these bits of description and ideas into advice to yourself? As you read, make notes about how what the teacher says applies to your own situation.

****

Teacher One: What worked for me was to be quiet and firm with my discipline. My most effective tool, however, turned out to be my weird sense of humor. Students would expect me to come off strict at certain times and I would throw them off by using humor to gain class control. This was not used all the time. Students will also listen to the tone of your voice; if you sound like you mean business, they will take you seriously. One important tip is to stand your ground.

****

Teacher Two: Let students have a hand in the decision making. Make deals with students and have them accept the deal openly.

****

Teacher Three: The louder my voice gets, the louder the students' voices get. To be completely silent and wait for them is much more effective than saying, "Quiet, please." When silence is used, students on your side will do the "quiet, please" for you.

****

Look back at the tips for management. Choose five that you would support. List reasons why you think these would be good tips. List those that you think would not work. Again, give reasons why these are poor tips.

Teacher Four: My English 23 class had a problem keeping on task early in the unit. I clued into the fact that they enjoyed listening to music while completing assignments. I used this to my advantage and the class and I made a deal. Whenever they were asked to complete a written assignment in class, if they were honestly working hard, they were allowed to listen to whatever kind of music they wanted. This worked so well with this group that I only once had to take away this privilege.

****

Teacher Five: I established management expectations immediately. I was their teacher first and their friend second. I loved class management because it flowed for me. The kids responded well to a couple of basic rules: 1) respect for everyone, and 2) respect for learning. These rules encompassed everything and also provided an arena for freedom.

****

Teacher Six: What worked for me was being mellow, being able to laugh at myself and others, allowing "human space" — non-disruptive motion/chatter, recognizing that control should never be absolute, and doing something wacky to get attention (standing on a desk, speaking with an accent).

MY WORST CLASS

ONE OF THE POINTS WE HAVE BEEN TRYING to make and review in this chapter and throughout the book is that, in teaching, no matter how great a teacher you are not everything goes well. The following six stories are about teachers who, while they are good teachers, have made mistakes. As you read these stories, jot down ideas that help you figure out just what the teachers' mistakes were and what could be done about them.

****

Teacher One: One of my worst classes was the grade ten class where I tried to talk about character in the short story "The Parsley Garden." I had tremendous trouble with classroom discipline in the class and I think that is the major reason I didn't feel good about it. I was explaining the difference between static and dynamic characters; I felt that the character was dynamic and the kids disagreed with me. We argued it back and forth and it was just gross. I felt very frustrated and I felt like I wasn't getting my point across at all. I felt as if I had no control, like they thought I was stupid and that they all hated me.

****

Teacher Two: My English 20 class had just finished acting Act IV of Macbeth before spring break. After the break, I wanted to quickly review the important parts of the scene and go on. I had gone through this identical process for Act III,

with success. But this time it was terrible! People weren't able to answer even simple questions about the events of the scenes. I got very frustrated when I realized that I had to backtrack, and my frustration (regrettably) showed. I think doing the same thing twice in a row (acting) was a bad idea — the class was much less interested in doing it a second time, and responded accordingly.

****

Teacher Three: My worst class was probably my introductory class to *The Rime of the Ancient Mariner.* I decided to show the film version first as a general introduction to the poem. Unfortunately I did not anticipate that the students would have such a hard time with the archaic language of the poem. They really didn't have a clue what was going on. This created a very negative first impression of the poem, which I was unable to completely overcome in subsequent classes. I felt a little frustrated by the students' negativity but then I realized that it was my fault so I felt very badly that I had done such a poor job introducing them to the poem.

****

Teacher Four: Students were working in groups. The noise level was fairly high yet on-task. I had to get the students back into rows while I gave instructions for presenting during the last ten minutes of class. The class was much too loud, and I couldn't get them under control. I yelled. I felt helpless and stressed, and also embarrassed — the good students realized I couldn't do much.

****

Teacher Five: The first class back after spring break we had to grade two assignments: 1) spelling sheets from class and 2) handouts from the short story *The Moose and the Sparrow.* Only half the class had completed the short story handouts, and less than half had done the spelling handouts. Frustrated, I decided to begin a lesson and instead grade both during the next class.

****

Teacher Six: I taught a grade eight class fairly early in the term and it was chatter, chatter, chatter from the word "go." I tried low-key management strategies but nothing seemed to work. Finally, I lost it and blew up at them. First I was yelling, and then I switched tactics to the "I'm so disappointed in you," speech. By the end of the period I had students apologizing and writing notes of apology as well. I felt like a raving lunatic. Something snapped and I lost it. Then I started to feel like I really wanted to make a difference.

MY BEST CLASS

OF COURSE, SOMETIME THINGS GO VERY WELL. Then the job of teaching becomes fun, exciting, and actually takes on a glow. The following six stories are about teachers who remember the successes of their classrooms. As you read these stories, jot down ideas that help you figure out why the classes went so well.

****

Teacher One: During a Science 10 period, a mature and intelligent class discussion took place. I taught briefly and outlined my expectations. The culmination of much work that was done both in and out of class was a videotape. It was very effective and introduced different dynamics. It was very creative and productive.

****

Teacher Two: My English 13 class showed a lot of energy during the Texas Scramble. The students showed they were willing to try new things and take risks. There was good communication and they knew what the assignments were and when they were due.

****

Teacher Three: Making a peanut butter sandwich as part of a lesson on following directions was my best class. I wanted my students to be aware of the importance of precise directions so I developed a mini-lesson where I made a peanut butter sandwich as the students gave me directions. I did exactly what they said and it turned out to be a very enjoyable lesson for both them and me. My students enjoyed the lesson so much that all day, students from other classes were asking if they were going to make peanut butter sandwiches in class too.

****

Teacher Four: I arranged for group work cooperative note taking, where the students recorded the information on a chart and then a spokesperson presented the information. This class went very well. The students worked well in groups and they had no problem presenting their information. This class was good because the students were on task. They appeared to enjoy what they were doing and they also learned as was evidenced through their presentations.

****

Teacher Five: My best class was actually a series of classes in which I was not actually "teaching." In these lessons my grade nine classes were working on their poetry projects. I spent these classes wandering around answering questions, discussing poetry and other things with the students, making sure they had everything they needed to do their project. I had successful classes teaching in front of the entire class, but I feel I did my best teaching during these informal, one-on-one situations. I really got to know the kids very well through these moments.

****

Answering the Tough Questions

Throughout this chapter, we have listed question after question. Probably you thought these were part of the narrative. Not. Reread the questions in this chapter. Pick five that you think you know the answers to — your answers. Pick five that you really have some difficulty answering. For these ten questions, outline some answers (about 1/2 a page each). When you are finished, share and discuss your outlined answers with another student. What insights did you gain from this discussion?

Teacher Six: This may not be my best class, but I do have one enduring memory. Lanny Thomas was a tall young junior high school girl. I always thought she was a very attractive and intelligent young woman, but she always felt like her height (she was over 6 feet tall) made her stick out like a sore thumb. All year, it seemed, I worked hard to encourage her — for one thing noting all the beautiful women in the world who were over 6 feet tall — but it seemed to no avail. At the end of the year, a note appeared on my desk. It was from Lanny. "Thank you for a good year," it said. "When I first started the year I thought I wanted to kill myself. Now I know I won't."

A FINAL WORD

CLASSROOM MANAGEMENT is one of the biggest fears that any beginning, and many experienced teachers have. It is true that management is a problem. Any time you get more than thirty dynamic young people together, you are going to have action, and noise, and rule breaking. If you went into teaching expecting that students would be "good," you will be disappointed over and over again.

However, in many ways, you will come to like the dynamic, active, and unruly nature of your students. They keep you hopping; they are always a surprise; and life is never boring in the classroom. One experienced teacher we know once said "Kids will surprise you. Just when you think that they couldn't frustrate you more than they are, they will prove to you that they can.

So, what can a teacher do? The one bit of advice that we have given over and over again in this chapter is to try to solve problems before they happen. Instead of focusing on the bad, focus on the good. During your regular classroom activities, include ideas for interacting positively with students. Then, don't sweat the little things. You know that there will be problems. Expect them. Remember it isn't always your fault. Fix the things you can, and don't worry about the things that are out of your control. Teaching, like golfing, can be fun — but you have to keep the right attitude.

CHAPTER 5

APPROACHES TO TEACHING

INTRODUCTION

TO BE OF ANY PRACTICAL USE, any discussion of teaching styles must be rooted in theoretical assumptions about learners and their development. In other words, it would be impossible for us to write about teaching styles without considering how learners learn. That is one reason why this chapter follows a chapter on learning. Your own teaching style will depend, in part, upon the beliefs and understandings you have of teaching. It will also depend, in part, on your personality and the natural way you learn best. And, it will depend in part on the students you teach — at least it should.

Most teachers mirror their learning in their teaching. That is, they implicitly understand how they learn and spend time trying to help their students learn in the same way they did. It's hard to blame teachers for working this way. It's what they know how to do. It's what they know will be successful. After all, the implicit belief at work is that "what's good for me is also good for others." It sounds self-centered, but it's completely understandable. Without thinking much about how we act as teachers, we set up experiences for students in our classrooms that we would like to experience. That's the natural way; it's quite understandable, and it's difficult to break out of it. Filling out the following chart will help you understand how you would (would like to) set up experiences for your students.

Teacher Strategy	Student Tasks	Teacher Work	Beliefs about Teaching	% of Time Used in Your Experience
1. Lecture (note taking)				
2. Seat Work (worksheet)				
3. Large Group Discussion				
4. Guest Speakers (other presentations — movies)				
5.				
6.				
7.				

THEORETICAL POSITIONS

IN ORDER TO REVIEW TEACHING STYLES, we need to first begin with a brief overview of some educational foundations. The beliefs and understandings of teachers have been greatly influenced by three different theoretical positions. The first belief was suggested by Rousseau and Freud who implied that the learner's mind is neutral and operates in a passive to active way. Because this was held to be true, the main focus in teaching should be the addition of new ideas to a subconscious store of old ones. Key instructional strategies will include lecturing and rote memorization.

The second belief was put forward by Skinner and Locke who suggested that the learner's mind is neutral and passive, but has innate reflexes and needs. The teacher's main focus should be to create the kind of systematic, successive changes in the learner's environment that increase the possibilities of desired behavioral responses. Repeated practice and reinforcement would be strategies employed by teachers using this understanding of learners.

The third belief was put forward by Dewey, Bruner, and Piaget. These educational theorists believed that learners were interactive and purposive individuals who were in continual interaction with their environments. The teacher's main task should be to help the learner gain new perceptions that lead to desired behavioral changes and that ultimately lead to a more fully functioning individual. Discovery and inquiry learning are key aspects of this approach to teaching.

YOUR TEACHING STYLE

WHAT THEORETICAL UNDERSTANDINGS influence your views of teaching? Have you considered the theories listed above? If so, do you subscribe to any one of them? Or do you think that good learning should be a combination of them all? How do your beliefs shape and influence your own classroom presence and teaching style?

No two teachers are ever alike and, similar to students, they also have their own learning styles. All of you will develop your own teaching style. More than likely, you will develop a variety of teaching styles, depending upon the classroom situation you have created or are facing.

The teaching style you adopt will be affected by a variety of factors. Some of the personal factors that will affect your teaching style will include:

1. How you view the learning environment.

Are you generally a positive, welcoming person? Are you business-like? Do you like to give clear expectations, or do you prefer to be a bit ambiguous as a way to encourage your students to be more creative? Will you allow student control over pacing and involvement? Will you accept what they want? Do you want students to "do it your way?" Do you want clearly attainable goals identified? Are you an approachable teacher, or are you a bit aloof?

2. How you plan your lessons.

Do you believe in thoughtful preparation, or do you like to provide a general structure and then "wing it?" Do you believe in clarity of learning expectations for students? Do you put relevance to students before the mandated curricular objectives? Do you like to account for the interest of students, linking of content to students' previous knowledge? Or are you more comfortable following the curriculum guide?

3. Your teaching behaviors.

Do you positively accept student responses, or are you teaching a curriculum that prizes conformity or one "best" way of doing things? Do you give "think" time to students, or do you prefer to deal with "first-draft" thinking and discussion? Do you present varying types of questions and expect a variety of answers? Are you comfortable with the natural enthusiasm and approachability of students, or do you prefer them to be well-managed? Are you aware of your own body language as well as that of the students? Do you like to use gestures, voice, and humor? Do you enjoy experimenting with a variety and flexibility of teaching strategies? Do you like to be continually aware of and monitor student activities? Are you organized or messy? Do you have the ability to attend to many things at once, or does juggling activities drive you crazy?

Finally, you must be aware of the nature of the learners you are working with and their preferential learning styles. If your teaching styles are flexible, you will be more able to create supportive and enabling learning environments for the variety of diverse students you will have in your classes. Beliefs and understandings about teaching translate into different teaching styles, each of which has merits and strengths. However, no teaching style is totally effective if used exclusively. A combination of different teaching styles is more likely to provide successful learning experiences for students.

A SPECTRUM OF STYLES

TRY TO ENVISION A SPECTRUM OF HOW TEACHERS and students act within a classroom. A teacher-centered and student-centered approach can probably be located at opposite ends of that spectrum. These two teaching approaches usually display some of the following characteristics:

Teacher-Centered Approach	Student-Centered Approach
autocratic	democratic
lectures (abstract learning)	group work, inquiry, discovery, reflection (related to student interests and experiences)
students seated in rows, seating arrangements face the front	seating arrangements vary
product focus	process focus
problem-solving — one correct response	problem-solving — multi correct responses
teacher choice	student choice
competitive learning	cooperative learning
teacher evaluation	peer coaching, self-evaluation

1. Direct Instruction

Direct instruction is the most traditional and teacher-centered form of instruction. In direct instruction, the teacher is the major information provider and usually presents information by lecturing, explaining, giving examples, and by providing students with opportunities for practice and feedback. Often students in these classrooms note that teachers who instruct directly "know their stuff."

Unfortunately, direct instruction can be boring. However, this does not have to be the case. Some direct instruction lectures are multi-faceted presentations which are both entertaining and informative. Most direct instruction requires large amounts of teacher talk and lesser amounts of teacher-student interactions. These interactions are often in the form of questions and answers, review and practice, and the correction of student errors.

The strength of direct instruction is that it is efficient. This is particularly true if the goal of a lesson is to present information. Direct instruction is also important when the lesson goal is achieving content mastery and when the learning of fundamental facts, rules, and sequences (like mathematics, grammatical conventions, or gaining a sight word vocabulary in reading) may be essential to subsequent learning.

Mastery learning may include some elements of more indirect and self-directed approaches such as group interaction and individual pacing. However, in mastery learning the teacher is usually involved in directing what information will be learned and in the criteria for how students will learn it. There is some flexibility in mastery learning, but this is generally limited to the amount of time allotted to students. Some students need more time than others if they are to learn the material the teacher determines is most important.

However, there are times when direct instruction strategies are not appropriate. Sometimes your teaching objectives do not focus on learning facts, rules, and behavior sequences. For example, if you want to help your students learn more complex cognitive skills such as the analysis, synthesis, and evaluation levels of Bloom's Taxonomy, direct instruction would actually hinder your students' ability to gain these skills. Practice in critical thinking is the key to these "higher levels" of skills; students cannot learn analysis, or synthesis, or evaluation well by having someone tell them. In these cases, learning by doing is the key.

Direct instruction would also be inappropriate when you want to present material that must be learned gradually over a long period. Direct instruction is also inefficient when you want to present information to students who have already mastered the basics of a given set of materials. When direct instruction repeats what has already been instructed, the experience can be stifling and boring for students.

As a teacher, you will find that redundancy and repetition are helpful, but the redundancy must be what we have termed "creative redundancy." The phrase creative redundancy simply means that you know that students need to have things repeated if they are to learn them well. However, if you repeat the content in the same, exact way all the time it is excessively boring. The trick in teaching is to repeat content in novel ways. For example, you may repeat a bit of factual infor-

Answering the question "Why do most teachers opt for direct instruction?" is not difficult. Most teachers want control and power in their classrooms. Direct instruction provides this opportunity. Teaching is a fearful job. People may say it's not true, but if a teacher is good that teacher will protect himself or herself by building a sort of fortress in the front of the classroom. The theory is simple: if you talk long and loudly enough, eventually the students will succumb.

The above statement was made by a teacher. What do you think? Take a side. Critique the statement. What do you believe about direct instruction?

On the face of it, competition in the classroom would seem to be a very negative thing. However, there are those who support the use of competition. Many believe that students should be taught how to live in a society that is, itself, competitive.

Is the competitive classroom really an educational system we want to support? Some say no; but some say yes. However, most people, including teachers, seem to accept competition as a given in the classroom. It's neither good nor bad; it's just the way life is in school.

Those who oppose competition point to its many problems. For example, competition can and does put pressure on students. In competitive classrooms, cheating is common. It is especially common among high school students where the ends are seen to justify the means. In such a situation, winning is everything.

Teachers, if aware of pressure-packed situations, can bring a calming influence to the classroom. In these cases, teachers need to encourage students to focus on learning rather than on winning and on the fun aspects of competition rather than on the serious aspects. In the best scenario, competition is a fundamental aspect of all games. If it is kept at the level of game playing, competition can be energizing and no one gets hurt. But, at its worst, competition can damage young students — sometimes beyond repair.

What do you think about competition in a classroom? How much will you use it? Do you think you can understand the negative effects of competition? Are these real to you or are they simply theoretical concepts? In other words, you probably would not be in here in university if you had not been the

mation through a lecture, through a story, through a game, through a crossword, through answering questions, or on an examination.

An unexpected and unwanted side effect of direct instruction can be student competition for grades. Competition can add flavor and, at least in our experience, seems to touch a basic human need. However, the problem with competition is that it can take the focus off learning and put it completely on grades. If this happens, the students no longer care about the knowledge they will learn, they only come to care about the grades they receive. Such a focus perverts the idea of education.

Another problem with excessive competition is that it can shape the way a teacher views the worth of students. Teachers who believe that student worth has some correlation to grades soon come to value students who get good grades more than those who do not. It would be almost impossible not to. Competitive learning exists when student goal attainments are viewed negatively in relation to other students' goal attainments. In other words, competitive learning is similar to competitive society; it has the potential to pit one student against another as each competes for limited resources — in this case grades. And as in society, one "winner" means many failures.

2. Indirect Instruction

Indirect instructional methods differ from direct teaching methods. Instead of a teacher efficiently attempting to pass on specific information, facts, or rules to students — usually through some sort of lecture presentation — teachers who use indirect approaches present instructional stimuli to students in the form of content, materials, objects, and events, and ask students to go beyond the information they are given to make and test their own conclusions and generalizations. In other words, these teachers engage students in an event or activity that creates an environment where they think the students have to learn the material.

Students become involved in activity, creating ideas, testing their own conclusions, discussing what they see and experience. By making and testing their own conclusions and generalizations, students can discover patterns of relationships. Student response to indirect instruction can take many different forms. However, there is rarely a single best answer. Instead, the student is guided to an answer that goes beyond the problem or stimulus material presented. The student may then be asked to rigorously challenge this answer, so that it might be tested against another more difficult critique. In this process, the student is pushed to develop advanced levels of thinking that will withstand the rigor of outside challenge.

The most distinctive difference between direct and indirect instruction is that direct instruction works best when it is about a particular product — a specific thing (a fact, for example) that is learned. Indirect instruction works best when it is about a process — a way of learning. Some teachers only teach directly. They lecture; they assign students readings or questions to answer; they use skill and drill, or worksheets, or fill-in the blanks. One of the reasons they utilize direct instruction is that they are more comfortable with control and structure. They desire efficient instruction; they hate wasting time. They view indirect instruction and they dislike the waste. "You can't control what the students learn," they say. "There is a specific curriculum and I am responsible for it. How can I know that the students will learn what I want them to know if I don't present it to them. That's my job."

These teachers are right: it is impossible to control what students learn. You can set up a situation where you think that students can't possibly miss what you present, but they will. As the old saying goes, "You can lead a horse to water, but you can't make it pick up the gold that twinkles just in front of its nose when drinking." On the other hand, indirect instruction is expansive learning, and it includes the teacher as a learner as well. The students are dynamic, with minds of their own. They will see and point out things that you would have never expected and that you would have never seen. Guess what? They can teach you.

We like indirect instruction better. We like teaching because we like learning. We keep teaching because it allows us to keep learning. We have wonderful jobs, and we admit it. We have learned a lot from our students. Sure, there is a curriculum. Sure, there are specific things that students are mandated to learn. But, if the students don't learn those things indirectly, we will return to the site of the gold in the stream and reteach the points, using direct instruction if necessary. We're not above cleaning up an academic mess. In addition, we just think that indirect instruction is more fun.

If you choose to make your instruction more indirect, there are a variety of ways that you can structure how you work. Some of the more common techniques of indirect instruction include:

1. providing advance organizers and conceptual frameworks to guide students as they look at materials,
2. using examples and non-examples so that students can examine and test patterns and categories of thinking,
3. using questions to guide the search and discovery process,
4. encouraging students to use examples and references from their own experiences so that they can come to understand what they do not know by comparing it to what they do know,
5. helping students evaluate themselves so they can understand how they can improve, and
6. using discussions to encourage critical thinking such as examining alternatives, judging solutions, making predictions, and discovering generalizations.

3. Discussion

Discussion is a strategy that is often mis-represented in classrooms. The best discussions are interactive dialogues between teachers and students, where any of the parties can move the discussion down different avenues of learning. However, what is often said to be discussion is little more than a question and "go-fishing" answer period, where the teacher is in control of the "correct" answers and the goal is to test the students' level of factual learning.

The problem with indirect teaching is that it's an excuse for teachers not having a clue what is going on in their classrooms. Often indirect teaching means the same thing as being out of control or flying by the seat of your pants. In any classroom, someone has to be in charge: that person is the teacher. Unfortunately, those teachers who promote indirect instruction also tend to promote permissiveness.

The above statement was made by a teacher. What do you think? Take a side. Critique the statement. What do you believe about indirect instruction? Make sure you think about and list the good and bad points of both direct and indirect instruction.

Not all teachers are interested in using discussions. In order to use either large or small group discussion in class successfully, teachers must be prepared to learn as much as they teach. A real discussion can be frightening because the teacher chooses to give up the entire control of the classroom, and there is a chance that the classroom can become uncontrollable as students get excited about what they are talking about. A discussion will not always go in the direction you anticipate, and you may not be able to "cover" all the issues or items that you had intended. This lack of coverage can be problematic.

Furthermore, a teacher who uses a discussion method must be willing to accept all genuine student responses, even those that are immature (as students often are) and in first-draft (which often happens when students are considering and stating new ideas verbally for the first time). Teachers who use discussion must be open-minded enough to consider student perspectives. Students will not always agree with you, but that does not make their points less valuable or less important. If you want to give students time for discussion, you must be prepared to guide them rather than manipulate the direction of the dialogue in the way you want it to go. Such a stance may sound easy, but it is not. Students can be very expressive.

4. Cooperative Learning

Although the phrase "cooperative learning" is a recent addition to educational jargon, the ideas of cooperative learning are old. Cooperative learning strategies generally work well with indirect teaching styles. Basically, cooperative learning is a strategy that encourages a combination of collaboration, competition, and independence. Teachers structure interdependence among students by encouraging them to attain their learning goals while interacting with each other.

The strengths of cooperative learning include its social nature. Instead of having to "be quiet," students are actually encouraged to share with each other. And, if handled well, the very activity of cooperative learning can help reduce the students' needs to talk with each other — which we believe is a basic human activity. If the social aspect of talking with each other is seen as positive instead of negative, many of the little distractions of the classroom can be placed aside and accepted as part of the classroom activity. In other words, we believe that one of the up-sides of cooperative learning is that the classroom may become a bit noisier, but classroom management gets easier. The teacher can accept some off-topic chatting as part of the social activity of cooperation. Think about it. Adults both work and socialize all the time; one does not preclude another.

In an academic sense, cooperative learning gives students opportunities to develop high levels of conceptual reasoning and problem-solving skills. Cooperative learning includes five basic situations:

1. situations where students learn positive interdependence,
2. situations which provide face-to-face interaction among students,
3. situations where individual students are accountable for mastering the assigned material,

4. situations where interpersonal and small-group skills are appropriately developed and used, and
5. situations where students are able to process how well the learning groups are functioning and are able to become involved in reflection and goal-setting.

Most proponents of cooperative learning state that cooperative learning has had widespread and powerful effects on instructional outcomes and encourage teachers to use it frequently. They also believe competitive and individualistic learning may still have a place in classrooms, but believe that these techniques should be used to supplement and enrich the cooperation among students. Proponents state that students will compete more positively with one another after cooperative experiences — it's easier to lose against people that you know and like.

Research suggests that students believe they experience more success in classrooms that use cooperative methods as opposed to classrooms that use competitive or individualistic learning situations and in these cooperative situations motivation is more intrinsic. Cooperative learning has also been shown to create warmer relationships among students and a more positive attitude toward the subject area. If you choose to teach cooperatively, your role as teacher will include:

1. clearly specifying the lesson's objective,
2. deciding students' group placements beforehand,
3. clearly explaining the tasks and goal structure to the students,
4. monitoring the effectiveness of the groups and intervening to provide assistance when necessary, and
5. evaluating your students' achievement and helping them discuss how well they collaborated with each other.

As mentioned earlier, it is important to teach students how to work collaboratively. It may seem odd, but most students need to learn how to communicate and build a trusting climate. It seems like this skill should come naturally, but it does not. Teaching cooperatively does not mean that students will never disagree. On the contrary, almost anyone involved in serious educational situations will disagree with each other. But in cooperative classrooms disagreement can also be a positive circumstance for further learning.

When members of a group disagree, they should be aware that, if they follow some basic ideas of academic etiquette, disagreement is not in itself a problem. Some of the rules and methods we would encourage you to adopt before disagreement occurs are: (1) use a problem-solving approach, (2) be critical of ideas, not people, (3) explore all views, then synthesize these views to arrive at a best solution, and (4) work to understand other perspectives. These skills are instructive to life far beyond school.

In cooperative classrooms, you must carefully consider the criteria for grouping students and the way the groups will be organized. Will students be allowed

Observe a class discussion and record all of the questions posed by the teacher. After the discussion, put all of the questions into categories depending on their level (knowledge, comprehension, etc.) Also record the number of seconds that the teacher waited for a student to answer each question. What differences could you note when sufficient rather than insufficient wait time was given? Did students respond in different ways when they were given adequate time to respond? Did students respond differently to more difficult rather than to simpler questions? What other observations did you make during this discussion?

ACTIVITY:

Design an activity for your particular subject area that attends to each of the five situations listed above. In one paragraph for each situation, create all the circumstances you need to do the lesson content.

Grading, like it or not, is part of teaching. In any group situation, cooperative or not, the teacher should assign and communicate grades to the students. Grades may be given in a number of ways for cooperative situations. Some of these ways include:

1. average members' individual scores
2. total the members' individual scores
3. assign a group score on a single product
4. randomly select one member's paper to score
5. randomly select one member's exam to score (all group members certify that each has mastered the material being studied)
6. individual score plus group bonus (for achieving a preset criterion by all group members)
7. bonus points based on lowest score
8. individual score plus group average
9. average of academic scores plus collaborative skills performance score
10. dual academic and non-academic rewards

to select their own groups? Will you select groups randomly, or will groups be based on student personality or academic ability? Will you expect all students to work in groups, or will you allow students to work independently? How long will the groups be expected to work together? Will you continually monitor, intervene, and evaluate the groups' effectiveness, or will you leave them alone to work out any problems that might come up? Will you use formal observation sheets, or will students be taught to observe and evaluate their own group performances in an informal manner?

5. Self-Directed Instruction

As students become more mature learners, they should be encouraged to actively engage in the learning process with self-directed instructional approaches. Active participation should be expected from all students; without it students become too dependent on the teacher. All students need to develop higher level reasoning, critical-thinking, and problem-solving skills.

Metacognitive strategies (mental processes used by the learner to understand the content and the approaches being taught, such as self-interrogation, self-assessment, analyzing, and memory aids for classifying and recalling information) are often used by students who have grown to an academic maturity that helps them become independent. These metacognitive strategies can be modeled by the teacher who (1) shows students the reasoning involved and (2) focuses students on applying the reasoning.

Teachers who use self-directed approaches to learning (1) provide information to the students about when and how to use mental strategies for learning, (2) explicitly illustrate how these strategies can be used to think through solutions to real-world problems, (3) encourage students to go beyond the material presented, or restructure it to their own way of thinking, (4) shift the responsibility of learning to the student through question-and-answer dialogue and discussions, and (5) monitor and correct student responses as such correction is needed.

In self-directed learning, perfection can become a problem. Good students need to make mistakes and learn from them. Functional errors may be inaccurate, but they are meaningful ways to learn. These errors can enhance the learner's understanding of content and provide a logical steppingstone for the next level of understanding. Reciprocal teaching (where learners instruct each other) can be used to give students opportunities to explore the content to be learned through classroom dialogue and group discussions. In discussions where the learning is truly reciprocal, the teacher and students naturally take turns directing the discussion. Predicting, questioning, summarizing, and clarifying are four reciprocal teaching activities. These activities help the teacher gradually shift the responsibility of learning to the students.

COOPERATIVE VERSUS COMPETITIVE LEARNING

EARLIER WE TALKED about cooperative learning as if it were the best possible teaching method. However, cooperative learning can produce its own classroom management problems. There is something to say for the impact of competitive, individualized, or competitive goal structures. These structures can promote and encourage a student's attention. Certainly, we would not deny the fact that facing down a difficult exam encourages students to study; and we see nothing wrong with encouraging students to work.

There are teaching methods that we would never use because we believe that are always immoral; however, competition is not one of them. Like most things, competitive methods can help you, as a teacher, motivate the learning of your students — which is your job. But these competitive and individualistic methods can be, and often are, overused. When skillfully used, and when used in moderation, the structures of competition and individualism can motivate learners, can reduce some of the causes of discipline problems, and can help ensure that discipline problems are not compounded. For us, one of the keys is that the student should not be in competition with other students; instead, students should set their sights on conquering the content of the curriculum and the skills that go along with this content.

However, despite these points being made, we do promote cooperative learning structures because we believe they can be a real benefit to disruptive, non-responsive, unmotivated, depressed, shy, isolated, and disliked students. People who cooperate with each other exert and accept influence from each other. Students who learn to value differences become more accepting of others. When acceptance rather than rejection becomes common, inappropriate competition is generally eliminated. We like to talk with our friends and believe that students do, as well.

If you want to become a good teacher, we believe you must be willing to experiment. You must also accept the fact that developing more effective procedures is a continuous process. But no situation is error-proof. Barriers and problems will always arise in classrooms. You will change and your students will change with you. As you grow as a teacher, the more strategies you learn to use and become comfortable in using, the more likely you will be able to offer success-oriented lessons to all of your students. Remember, that's your job — to help your students learn.

FIVE OBSERVATION ACTIVITIES THAT WILL HELP YOU VIEW TEACHING

Activity One: Observing Teacher Clarity

Directions: Observe a teacher presentation for clarity using the following indicators. Were objectives clearly stated? Was the organization of the lesson made explicit? Were appropriate examples used? Were transitions used to move from one point to the next? Were students checked with to verify understanding? Was a variety of media used to accommodate various learning styles? Record specific examples of clarity of presentation, and consider why these examples were clear.

Activity Two: Observing Teacher Enthusiasm

Directions: As you observe a teacher giving a presentation, check the following elements of enthusiasm. How was voice used? Was eye contact made? Were gestures used? Describe the teacher's facial expression. What emotions were conveyed to the students about the content of the presentation? What words were selected to present the material? How were questions and ideas accepted by the teacher? What was the overall level of energy? Was enthusiasm conveyed to the students in other ways? How do you convey enthusiasm about the material you are presenting? How could you make your own lessons more animated and exciting for students?

Activity Three: Assessing Teaching Performance

You can use the following questions to assess your own teaching performance if you videotape a lesson, or you can use them to assess a lesson you observed one of your peers teaching. This particular observation activity relates to a cooperative learning lesson. Consider which aspects of the lesson were well presented and which aspects need to be improved.

Was the content appropriate for the lesson?
Were the plans for team formation effective?
Were the materials able to support the lesson effectively?
Did the teacher seem to be prepared?
Were the goals and purposes well explained?
Was assistance given to the students in their groups?
Was individual and group effort recognized appropriately?

Activity Four: Observing Small Group Interaction

How capable were the students of working in small group situations? How much were they on-task, and what activities were they engaged in when they were working — reading, discussing, recording, observing? How did the teacher's actions and directions contribute to the on-task behaviors? How much were they off-task? What could the teacher have done to prevent this lack of working or lack of understanding?

Activity Five: Observing the Roles of a Teacher

Directions: Accompany a teacher for a day. As you observe throughout the day, record all teacher activities and estimate the amount of time that each takes. Also record, as best as you can, how the teacher feels about doing each of the activities. At the end of your observation day, categorize the activities into five categories (organizing, presenting, planning, evaluating, and managing the classroom). Which activities took up most of the teacher's time? Which ones appeared most enjoyable? Least enjoyable? How could the teacher's time be used more productively, in your view?

TEACHING LEARNING STRATEGIES

WHEN TEACHERS ENTER CLASSROOMS, they have two kinds of goals (1) to teach students how to learn (process) and (2) to help students achieve the products or content of learning. Successful teaching requires a teacher to be sensitive and skillful in achieving both types of goals.

You can help students become successful learners by creating methods and strategies that facilitate learning. As teachers, we sometimes take too much for granted. Sometimes we expect students to learn without teaching them **how** to learn. With a little thoughtfulness, you can create strategies that help your students not just learn, but learn how to learn. Some of these strategies include such things as imaging, summarizing, and note taking. If students can improve these very basic skills, they can improve their own ability to learn. You have set them up to be independent, mature learners instead of keeping them dependent upon you to provide them with the content. It may seem ironic, but the less you do for students as a teacher, the more they will learn to do for themselves. If you can give them the knives and forks of learning, soon they will be able to cut their own food.

In a practical way, can you imagine how this simple task can change the whole make-up of the classroom and the way that you, as a teacher, and they, as students, interact. The hierarchical status of teacher as big and learner as little can be eroded. In its place is a stronger, more appropriate structure of mutuality and cooperativeness. Cooperative learning is more than students cooperating; it can, and we think should, also involve teachers. We think classroom life works better when everyone is a learner.

> **Rehearsal strategies** help the learner pay attention to important aspects of what is being learned and to transfer the material into working memory. Students' spontaneous use of rehearsal strategies during learning increases with age, so that by age six or seven children are often able to use rehearsal strategies when instructed to do so, but are not able to generate useful strategies spontaneously. Some examples of rehearsal strategies include repeating the names of items in ordered lists (such as memorizing planets), repeating material aloud, copying

Observing the Roles of a Teacher

Directions: Accompany a teacher for an extended period of time. As you observe throughout the day, record all teacher activities and estimate the amount of time that each takes. Also record, as best as you can, how the teacher feels about doing each of the activities. At the end of your observation day, categorize the activities into five categories (organizing, presenting, planning, evaluating, and managing the classroom). Which activities took up most of the teacher's time? Which ones appeared most enjoyable? Least enjoyable?

material, taking selective notes, and underlining important parts of the text.

Elaboration strategies can also be useful learning strategies for students. Examples of elaboration strategies include (1) paired-associate learning, in which associations are built between a variety of items, and images can be connected with the associations, (2) paraphrasing, (3) summarizing, (4) creating analogies, (5) generative note taking, in which students learn how to distinguish between main and subordinate ideas, to abbreviate words, to paraphrase, and to use an outline format, and (6) question answering, so that students may integrate presented information with prior knowledge.

Organizational strategies require the learner to be actively involved in tasks such as clustering or organizing items on the basis of shared characteristics or attitudes, outlining and organizing material being studied, or breaking things into parts and then identifying the linking relations among the parts.

A FINAL WORD

WHEN WE BEGIN OUR UNIVERSITY CLASSES with teacher candidates, we ask these students to name the best teachers they have ever had and to tell the rest of their classmates the characteristics that made these people such memorable teachers. We then discuss this list of characteristics as a group. Over the years we have asked this same simple, but important question repeatedly. Some characteristics have emerged as typical of great teachers. These include a sense of humor, the willingness of teachers to take the time to really care in active and concrete ways, teachers who know their stuff, and teachers who build special personal relationships with students at a time when students have real needs.

This little list of characteristics of great teachers is worth storing in your box of memories. But, to us, the most striking thing about the characteristics of "best" teachers is that no one methodology or action or personality seems to dominate the best teacher list. Some students liked lectures; some liked teachers who used group work; some liked combinations. Great teachers, as a group, tend to have certain personality traits or character traits, but they also tend use very different methodologies.

What can we learn from these differences? Probably not to trust those books or "experts" who bring us some cure-all methodology — like behavioral objectives, cooperative learning, or inquiry teaching. Good teachers probably use all these activities. Or, maybe they don't. Honestly, we don't know and won't pretend to.

What we do know about teaching is that good teachers are hard-working, caring, "street-smart" people who shape their classroom environments in practical, dynamic ways. As we mentioned earlier, the job of the teacher is to help students grow to a place where the teacher is no longer needed. All worthwhile teaching styles share this goal.

CHAPTER 6

INCLUSIVE EDUCATION

INTRODUCTION

LIKE IT OR NOT, INCLUSIVE EDUCATION IS HERE. Inclusive education is the name for the educational movement to include all children, regardless of academic abilities or academic disabilities into regular classrooms. Typically, inclusion refers to the integration of students with special education needs into regular classrooms. The inclusive education movement has been supported by most parents, especially parents of special education students. These parents make the point that their children have the right to be educated in a regular classroom.

Inclusive education is one of today's educational "hot" topics, and there are a variety of positions on inclusive education. Positively stated, one goal of inclusive education is to help students and staff gain an understanding and an appreciation of all groups present in the local, national, and global communities. Negatively stated, inclusive education, or mainstreaming, means placing "special needs" students into regular classroom situations. Inclusion has generated a number of practical questions for teachers, who are faced with new and confusingly difficult roles and responsibilities. The whole "problem" of inclusion has been exacerbated by the fact that inclusion has not brought with it expanded support staff or funding. This lack of support has increased teacher dissatisfaction and frustration.

We agree. The teachers we have spoken with about inclusion have talked openly about the difficulties of teaching in an inclusive classroom. The reason we have used the term negative is because inclusive education has brought teachers a great deal of anxiety and extra work. However, there are some very positive aspects to the whole idea of integration. The purpose of this chapter is to explore some of the reasons for involving students with special needs in the classroom

In the situation we describe the school has obviously decided that its task is to educate the student by encouraging her to work to her academic potential and has all but ignored her social life. Often, newspapers write about young students who are so successful at academic learning that they have graduated from university at 13 years of age. Our society seems to celebrate these young people, calling attention to their genius. What do you think? How do you think the school should handle those people who are so obviously gifted in the ways of the school? Is it good to encourage students to attend university at the age of 11? Consider the variety of options that schools have. List some of these options. What are the good points and the bad points of any decision that could be made?

and to suggest ways to make this involvement more beneficial for teachers and other students. In other words, even if you don't like the idea of inclusive, you will be "facing it" as a teacher.

Many people, including some teachers, believe that mainstreaming means to bring students with special needs into "regular" classrooms with "normal" children. But there are some problems with this perspective. The first is that, as we have pointed out earlier in the book, there is no "regular" classroom with "normal" children. Children are never "normal." All children are unique. Because they are unique, they all have individual strengths and individual weaknesses.

In our experience, all children can perform well at some tasks. But schools are a unique culture with a unique set of rules. Most of us take this culture for granted because we are accustomed to it. In fact, as we have pointed out before, those of you who are reading this book are especially adept at living in this culture. If you were not, you would probably not have made the choice to become a teacher.

Schools have their own criteria for success and for failure. Given the criteria used to evaluate success in schools, some students are very "successful;" some are not so "successful." This does not mean, however, that those students who are not successful in school will not eventually find a place where they will be successful. We're sure that all of you have heard stories of famous intellects — people like Thomas Edison and Albert Einstein — who were busts in schools. The point we are making here is that schools have their own unique societies with their own unique rules. These two creative and wonderful thinkers just didn't fit.

When a child enters a school, that child becomes a student and must follow the rules that go along with being a student. In schools, all students are "ignorant" (meaning that there are areas that they have ignored) and all students have weaknesses (meaning that there are skills that they do not know and need to learn). Some children take to being students more easily than others. One young woman we know has been so adept at learning the curriculum — it comes so easy to her — that she needs individual challenges. The school has responded by placing her, alone, in the hall working on advanced, university-level material for almost all her subjects. She spends the day virtually by herself.

We believe that there are some basic truths to teaching. One truth is that all students need individualized attention to help them develop in particular areas. It should be no surprise that students have special needs. We all have special needs, and we can all benefit from personal and individual contact and support. Although teachers are expected to teach a class of thirty students all at once, as a teacher you need to remember that within this class you will be teaching thirty unique people. Although it is a difficult task, you should try to find ways to build success into each student's learning experiences.

SPECIAL NEEDS

ALL STUDENTS HAVE NEEDS, but some have more challenging needs than others. And some have to work much harder to achieve success than others. The tradition of North American schools, until recently, has been to exclude a variety of students from our regular public education systems. For example, students with severe physical and/or mental handicaps were placed in their own, "special" classrooms, quite separate from "regular" classrooms. The argument has typically been that it is more efficient to separate out those with difficult problems to a place where they can get "specialized help."

At the same time, North American schools have ignored the needs of gifted and talented students or only selected those students whose gifts and talents lay in "appropriate" areas. In the not-too-distant past, schools punished students with behavior disorders and learning disabilities. One of the reasons schools punished learning disorders was because it was difficult to recognize these difficulties. They became learning "problems," which meant classroom problems, because students with these "problems" created difficulties for teachers. So, although inclusive education does make teaching more difficult, there is an up-side. Today in our schools, we are working to become more aware of these students as a legitimate part of our society and we are trying to include them in regular classroom situations. To us, the more difficult teaching situations are worth it because for the first time students who were once thought of as "problems" are seen as having a legitimate place in the fabric of society.

Some people suggest, actually sometimes complain, that it is difficult to include children with special needs in all classrooms. They have a practical point. The more diverse the differences, the more difficult it is for a teacher to accommodate these differences. As schools accept more and more diversity in classrooms, teachers need to develop further strategies for individualizing instruction. We have already suggested the difficulties of providing this individual instruction. Developing these strategies takes a lot of extra time, especially when the life of a teacher is already so busy.

As we stated before, all students have needs. Some have "special" needs. What are "special needs?" How can we determine the special needs of students? If you are going to become a good teacher, we believe you must become aware of distinctions in students. If you can, you will find that knowing these distinctions will provide clues about how to teach your students with special needs more easily. The more you learn, the more you will be able to help yourself recognize and eliminate potential difficulties. Be warned, however. You will never be able to eliminate all the special problems you will face. Sometimes these problems are too difficult for you, as a teacher, to overcome. Sometimes you will have a hard time discovering these problems, no matter how hard you look. Students can be very good at hiding their needs. It often takes an extremely sensitive and experienced teacher to uncover what students are working to hide. For example, it took more than six months for one teacher to discover that a student in his classroom

We have been talking about how diverse a classroom can be, but how diverse actually is a classroom? It might be valuable now, in order to help you make sense of the types of diversity that might occur in any classroom, to take a minute to list all of the "special needs" you have observed in your own classroom experiences. When you have compiled this list, share it with others. As you share your list, try to suggest problems for children with these special needs in a classroom setting and discuss ways to accommodate special needs into a classroom setting. Instead of seeing the student as a problem, try to imagine how school is a problem for these students.

Think About It

What are some ways that teachers can begin to know their students more personally? How can teachers come to know their students as people rather than only as students? Or, is it important that teachers work to know students as people? What do you think?

had a severe hearing impairment. If that sounds impossible, let us assure you that it happened to one of the writers of this book.

As a teacher, you must be constantly aware of and sensitive to what students are telling you, even when they can't or won't use words. For example, are you aware of the reasons that a student squints consistently or has difficulty in pronouncing words clearly? Are comments that seem inappropriate said out of meanness, or are they the result of cultural differences or social inequalities? Are inappropriate actions caused from substance abuse or emotional difficulties? Do we know our students well enough to distinguish behavior or action that is markedly different from their normal behaviors or actions?

Before you can provide your students with effective learning experiences, we believe you need to know your students as multi-faceted human beings. As teachers, we need to learn about our students' intelligence, achievement, personality, and interests. We can, with the help of other professionals in the school (people like the counselor, learning assistance teachers, other classroom teachers, lunch supervisors, the administration, the school secretaries, and the janitors are all members of the team), identify individual student needs and use what we know about those needs to teach more effectively.

INDIVIDUALIZING INSTRUCTION

TEACHING TO STUDENTS WITH SPECIAL NEEDS and individualizing instruction go hand-in-hand. A teacher who hopes to address the special needs of students must see the classroom as a group of distinct students and must teach the class as a group of individuals — not as a class. So, how does a teacher individualize instruction? Some of the more typical, instructional strategies that individualize instruction include: (1) varying assignments in ways that take advantage of unique student abilities, (2) using verbal, visual, and kinesthetic techniques in presentations, (3) using cooperative learning activities like peer tutoring and small group learning, and (4) using interactive computer programs designed for individual students.

Like all teaching, the basic goal of teaching students with special needs in mind is to develop learning aptitudes that will help students throughout their lives. Education in general, and schooling specifically, should be seen as long-term aptitude and attitude development that prepares individuals for life. Aptitude and attitude are broad concepts that subsume many individual differences. Some of these individual differences include: (1) intellectual abilities that include cognitive skills and competencies, (2) personality characteristics like enduring affective-emotional dispositions, and (3) cognitive styles like those individual propensities for processing information in one way or another that develop around the particular abilities or personalities of students. If you are going to be an effective teacher, you must adapt your teaching style to shift the focus toward areas of student strength where students can capitalize on their unique aptitudes and learn to overcome areas of weakness or inaptitude.

When you change your teaching style in response to what you assess your students' readiness to be, you are helping your students become more successful in their learning. When this happens, teaching adapts to the students. To meet the needs of individual students, teachers can adapt, manipulate, and change the (1) organizational structures of the class (groups, learning centers, reward structures), (2) materials (examples, analogies, points of emphasis, reviews, summaries), (3) support materials (aides, media), (4) level and form of questions, (5) amount of time spent with individual students, (6) feedback, (7) pacing, and (8) evaluation to name a few. The point is that the entire classroom experience can and probably should change.

Students can also be helped to individualize their own learning. As they learn to take advantage of their own needs and aptitudes in learning, students become more mature learners. However, as we have said in the previous chapter, helping students become mature learners means that you cannot do everything for the students, making them more dependent on you rather than less dependent.

Becoming an independent learner is not always easy. First, students have been in schools; and schools, historically, have been places that typically encourage students to trust and follow the advice and the expertise of the teacher. Schools do not encourage students to think for themselves. To help students become independent learners means that you must structure your classrooms in ways that encourage independence.

Some strategies are more helpful in preparing students to become more independent learners than others. These strategies include: (1) providing a structured outline to students, so that they know what to expect, (2) teaching sequentially step-by-step, from concrete to more abstract , (3) checking frequently for comprehension to ensure that students are keeping up, (4) providing for over learning and adjust the pace accordingly, and (5) encouraging students to ask for individual extra help. These activities provide a positive structure that help students feel comfortable within a learning environment. Teaching independent learning does not mean abandoning students, just like teaching someone to swim does not mean throwing him or her into the deep water.

You need to be knowledgeable about the content you will teach and how it will be taught, but you also must learn how to adjust both content and teaching practices to the individual differences that exist among learners. Teachers need to understand the powerful effect that individual differences can have on learning, and they need to become more able to adapt or match instructional methods to the individual learning needs of our students.

Because not every student learns in the same way, you can help your students by (1) conducting student-centered discussions to improve the achievement of highly anxious students, (2) including some teacher-centered lecture classes that may improve achievement among low-anxiety students, and (3) alternating the approaches used (for example phonics or whole-word approaches when teaching reading).

Students have unique needs and strengths. Regardless of their specific needs, dealing directly with these differences means that teachers can (1) develop an understanding of the general characteristics of different types of students with special needs; (2) attempt to identify and meet the students' unique needs relative to this particular classroom; (3) design lesson plans that teach to different needs at the same time whenever possible; and (4) get assistance for providing appropriate instruction from the experts available (special education teachers) in developing individualized educational plans (IEPs) which state overall goals and objectives for each student and which design instruction to fit specific special needs.

IEPs can also be used for students with exceptional talents. Multilevel teaching can provide individualized instruction to groups of varying sizes and skill levels by (1) using the same materials to teach different objectives or (2) using different materials to teach the same objectives. Some steps to multilevel teaching include:

1. defining the objective for each skill and the sequence of steps necessary to teach each of these objectives
2. pre-testing each student to determine the entry level for a particular objective
3. preparing data sheets for recording performance during the instructional session
4. selecting materials that are easy to manipulate and adapt
5. presenting instructional tasks recording responses and other relevant information
6. analyzing the data after each session

HARD-WORKING STUDENTS

CLASSROOMS ARE DYNAMIC PLACES of high energy and excitement. They are always filled with students who bring not only a variety of abilities to the class but who also bring with them a variety of attitudes. Students who continually strive for success but have academic difficulties will need different educational experiences than those students who are reluctant to work hard.

Most students are not evil, nor are they lazy. Sometimes students have become discouraged with previous unsuccessful attempts. Most people can only try and fail so many times before they simply give up and quit. The real heroes of school are those young people who, despite a history of failure, keep on keeping on. And, in most circumstances, they deserve more help than they get.

So, how can you help these students? Some guidelines for helping students who are willing to work hard but continue to have difficulties include:
1. emphasizing basic communication skills (such as speaking, writing, reading)
2. working toward the improvement of basic reading skills (such as pronunciations, word meanings, comprehension)
3. teaching content in small sequential steps
4. varying instructional strategies often (as often as every ten minutes, depending upon your class)

5. using frequent comprehension class checks (as often as four during a class period)
6. using a variety of audiovisual and game materials to engage the visual, verbal, and kinesthetic learning modes
7. using frequent individual positive reinforcement, and working toward increasing the student's sense of personal worth
8. Ensuring that textbooks and other materials are at appropriate reading levels for students
9. Maximizing the use of supervised in-class, on-task work and minimizing the use of homework
10. Learning about each student and develop lessons around their interests, needs, and experiences
11. Becoming concerned with the students' successful understanding of content covered and their developing self-concepts rather than content coverage
12. Individualizing learning as much as possible (e.g., encourage oral expression for those limited in writing ability)
13. Teaching the skills of note taking, outlining, and listening

These guidelines also apply to students who are reluctant to work (regardless of their ability level). In addition, it is important for you to make your classroom rules and expectations clear at the beginning of the year and to follow through on what you say you will do. If you do not, the students may become confused or may come to disregard what you say. Students need help improving their study, learning, and behavioral skills if they are going to become more successful in school activities.

ATTENDING TO STUDENT DIFFERENCES

BECAUSE THERE IS SO MUCH TO LEARN AND CONSIDER, becoming a teacher is no easy task. It is one thing to note that there are student differences; it is another thing to know how to do something about these differences that will help students become better learners. Some student differences markedly affect their learning. These same differences cause teachers to view their jobs in different ways. Severe learning disabilities and mental or physical handicaps cause teachers to view learning and success in different ways.

Some of the important things you, as a teacher, need to consider are time, behavior, and communication. There are several different kinds of time. For example, engaged time means the length of time students are able to stay focused on a task. But there are also differences in the time some students take to learn something. You might, for example, give the same test to a group of students who all have similar knowledge. In fact, two students might receive the same grade on an exam. However, one student might finish the exam in 20 minutes; another might take

50 minutes. There may be little difference in their knowledge; however, there may be a great deal of difference in their ability or desire to work quickly.

Students have many differences, even outside of academic differences. For example, some students have been "well-schooled" at home in ways that help them fit into public behavior. Other students have few social graces. In other words, their social behavior is poor and they have never learned the simple ability to work effectively in groups, to communicate with the teacher, or to find appropriate ways to be recognized. As a result, to fulfill the common human need to be recognized and considered, they do stupid things. Why? Because they need to belong more than they need to follow the social rules. Some students have never learned good work habits, neatness, and the ability to organize. Some students probably never will. These differences obviously impact on what we, as teachers, can do and how we think.

The quality of the program in any school is the most important factor when integrating students with special needs into the regular classroom. But in the instruction of all students, three elements should be present in the program:

1. An appropriate learning environment. Special learners need to be accepted as unique individuals with very special talents, but with significant limitations. We cannot and should not pretend to understand what it is like to be "handicapped," nor should we patronize or show undue sympathy to the student for his or her "condition." These students should be treated the same as all other students in the classroom. All students, despite their needs, should be treated like all other students — in some ways. For example, all students should be given respect and shown that they are "okay."

Some teachers believe that they should "go easy" on students with learning problems. On the surface, such an act of "kindness" seems appropriate. But the practical problem is that going easy on some students means lowering standards and the human truth is that people typically respond to the standards expected of them. If you expect lower standards, you will typically get them. You should set reasonably high expectations and help the learner set realistic goals. Handicaps should not be used as excuses for failing to reach goals. A predictable and consistent schedule and set of routines provides external security for the learner with special needs.

2. A meaningful curriculum. The curriculum for each student in a class should be determined by the individual educational plan and should reflect (1) instruction that is linked to the present level of progress, (2) frequent assessment of progress in order to make adjustments, (3) a focus on the mastery of essential basic skills, (4) a provision for direct instruction, (5) a sequence and a continuity of instruction, and (6) individual pacing for each student.

3. Quality instruction. As previously mentioned, teachers should maximize learning time and structure learning so that individual success rate is high. Teachers should also provide individual corrective feedback at regular and frequent intervals.

Learning is always tied to a student's self-perception. Students who have a positive self-concept will learn; those with a poor self-concept will not learn. Self-concept will affect attitude, which will affect the willingness to work, which will affect how much and how successfully students will learn. Differences in student self-concept affect how actively students become engaged in the learning process. The idea is simple: students will never learn if they don't actively engage in learning.

SELF-CONCEPT

WHETHER THEY LIKE IT OR NOT, teachers have influence over the formation of students' self-concepts. The performance of effective teachers should be guided by a belief in the inherent value of the unique talents and contributions of each individual student. One way to improve a student's self-concept is to find and reflect back to that student the value of his or her unique talents and strengths. As teachers, we can do this by encouraging self-management skills that will lead to greater independence and task completion, using peer tutoring, pairing students with different strengths, using learning centers and microcomputer software, and using less formal classroom arrangements.

OUTSIDE FACTORS

THE HOME LIVES OF STUDENTS create differences that affect their learning. The family and society continue to put the responsibility for creating well-rounded individuals onto the schools. Schools and teachers play a sort of schizophrenic drama with the rest of society. On one hand, society expects miracles from schools and teachers. On the other hand, society is always dumping on schools and teachers — blaming them collectively for all sorts of sins and wrongdoings. One of the problems of teaching is the sort of Catch-22 situation in which teachers live.

Whether or not schools can shape individual students to the extent that the family and the society believe is a moot question. The fact is that teachers have accepted this assignment as part of their jobs. But teachers are not the only influence on the academic or social success of students. Research has attributed several factors in the home and in society to the level of success students are able to achieve in school. Television and home videos, single-parent families, poverty, the desire for consumer or material success, and the emphasis on leisure all contribute to the ways that students learn. For one student, the home situation can spur learning; for another, the same home situation can discourage attempts at learning. As we have said before, teaching students is a complex task.

Socioeconomic status creates large and important differences in the classroom and influences the achievement of students. However, many educators believe that intelligence can be altered through instruction. These educators further believe that classrooms are the logical place to develop intelligence. Some theories of intelligence believe that intelligence consists of three parts: (1) an individual's internal world; (2) the way in which an individual acquires knowledge, and (3) an individual's external world.

Given this construct of intelligence, certain characteristics can impede intelligent thinking or behavior. These include: lack of motivation, lack of impulse control, lack of perseverance, using the wrong abilities, the inability to translate thought into action, a lack of product orientation, the inability to complete tasks and to follow through, failure to initiate, fear of failure, procrastination, misattribution of blame, excessive self-pity, excessive dependency, wallowing in personal difficulties, distractibility and lack of concentration, inability to delay gratification, inability or unwillingness to see the forest for the trees, lack of balance between critical and creative thinking, and too little or too much self-confidence.

Considering this list, the classroom is the logical place to convey attitudes and behaviors that can help learners avoid these impediments to intelligent behavior. To reduce achievement differences as much as possible and to get lower socioeconomic status students ready to learn, teachers can do the following:

1. incorporate a variety of audiovisual aids and exploratory materials into the lessons
2. have high expectations
3. reward intellectual accomplishments
4. provide support and encouragement
5. help students expand their vocabularies and quality of language by providing access to newspapers, periodicals, and popular books
6. seek opportunities for lower socioeconomic students to talk about their experiences and realize that they have valuable contributions to make to the class

INTELLIGENCE

GARDNER (1993) HAS CONCLUDED that there is more than one type of intelligence. If a classroom is to work well, these different types of intelligence need to be recognized. Gardner suggests that there are seven intelligences:

1. musical intelligence,
2. bodily-kinesthetic intelligence,
3. logical/mathematical intelligence,
4. linguistic intelligence,
5. spatial intelligence,

6. interpersonal intelligence, and
7. intrapersonal intelligence.

Learning activities require different degrees of these component parts of intelligence. The problem with schools has typically been that the traditional curricula have focused on some of these intelligences while discounting others as being unimportant to successful academic learning.

As the fabric of our society changes there is more need than ever to consider alternative ways of viewing learning and success. Teachers can no longer assume that all students in our classrooms have the same backgrounds, beliefs, values, or understandings that we do. They often do not even share common understandings with each other. This fact does not mean, however, that education should not focus on some core curricula or some basic, ethical ideals. As teachers, we believe that all students should have, at least, the following experiences. Inclusive classrooms should especially be places where these basic educational opportunities exist:

1. equity — all students, regardless of social class and ethnicity, should experience an equal opportunity to learn in school,

2. acceptance — all students need to be guided to develop positive attitudes toward different ethnic groups,

3. power — students from victimized groups need to be taught decision-making and social action skills,

4. interdependency — all students need to acquire cross-cultural dependency and view themselves from the perspectives of different groups,

5. accommodation without assimilation — teachers need to help members of diverse ethnic groups learn how to participate effectively in two cultural frames — their own and that of the school, and

6. expansion — teachers should work to provide students with a range of ways of seeing, knowing, thinking, and being that enables them to break from their everyday experiences.

When creating lesson plans, we should keep these goals in mind. These are important goals for every student in every class. How can we structure lessons that consider these goals? What strategies might be useful in creating awareness in students without creating hostility and defensive behavior? How do we involve the community in achieving these goals? How do we uncover the hidden curricula (unintended learnings acquired through the values, norms, and practices of the institution) and address it with students and colleagues?

Each of us is "included" in some form of minority group and can learn from understanding different perspectives and points of view. Take a minute now to brainstorm a variety of activities and strategies that could connect to your subject area and promote the goals listed.

INCLUSIVE LANGUAGE

NCLUSIVE CLASSROOMS ARE JUST THAT — classrooms that embrace all students regardless of special education needs, social class, ethnicity, gender, or sexual orientation. Central to any inclusive classroom is the usage of language. Language is a powerful and sometimes dangerous tool that both reflects and shapes the atmosphere of any classroom. Students are not "special-needs students"; rather, they are students who have special needs. The emphasis must be on the individual and unique child rather than on the label. We believe it is crucial that teachers encourage and model inclusive language in their classrooms.

A FINAL WORD

NCLUSIVE EDUCATION DOES NOT ALWAYS WORK. Many factors have led to the failures of inclusion. These include a lack of planning, a lack of collaboration, and poor funding mechanisms for special education. Still, current trends indicate that schools are moving toward more inclusive practices and are attempting to educate the majority of students with exceptional needs into the regular education classroom.

Restructuring your classroom so that it reflects the best opportunities for inclusion can be a difficult job. Such restructuring will demand that you consider the factors that influence change. One of your most important jobs is to create an atmosphere and a culture for change that encompasses the school's physical surroundings and structures, the formal policies and rules of the school, the school's resources, your own attitudes and beliefs and those of the administration, and the relationships that are shaped as a result of the curriculum. There is a lot to think about.

If inclusive education is to work well, it must be supported by parents, students, and teachers. School leaders must also actively demonstrate their own conviction that full inclusion is positive, and they must express this conviction through their actions. Planning curriculum change and providing resources for that change involve planning and the provision of time, money, building space, personnel, and any other resources needed to educate all students in regular classrooms.

Clearly, inclusive education is here. Clearly, teaching in an inclusive classroom can be difficult. However, there are rewards for you as a teacher. We believe one of the highest rewards of teaching is to help others, especially students. Teaching students with disabilities, regardless of what those disabilities are, is rewarding.

The research on inclusive education is promising. The results of several studies on the "regular" students show that regular students do not suffer in developmental outcomes. Whether they are in an inclusive classroom or not, regular students seem to develop at the same rate. Furthermore, research suggests that when children with disabilities are in the class, the teacher does not spend any less time with regular students. In other words, research does not show any significant decrease in the development of regular students when they are in the same classroom as disabled students. However, these same studies show that inclusion has proved beneficial in promoting the personal and educational development of regular students. Inclusive classrooms seem to be classrooms where students can learn and grow. Certainly they are classrooms where new teachers have ample opportunities to learn their trades.

What we want teachers to remember about inclusive education is that the methodologies that work well in regular classrooms also work well in inclusive classrooms. Good teaching is good teaching. There is no doubt that the principles of good teaching may have to be "tweaked" in inclusive classrooms, but these principles do not change drastically.